Bible Notes

Skim the Entire Bible in a Few Hours Instead of Months

D1520932

Mike Stork

Bible Notes

Contact Email: mikestorkbible@gmail.com

Table of Contents

Bible Notes

Introduction

This is a study book – a tool – to help you ready the entire bible for yourself and to develop your own devotionals to meditate on.

There is no bigger joy than to discover something for yourself in the bible that strengthens your faith. I found things that answered the big questions I had had – Like how can one person die on a cross save me? That didn't make sense till I found the answer in Romans.

I found at least 80 things no one ever mentioned or shown me in the bible. I came to some new conclusions on my own that I later found to be confirmed by bible scholars.

I pray and hope that you discover as much from the bible as I have on my own – I leave very little commentary but rely on you to teach yourself. I printed out my notes on every chapter of the bible – this helped me make better sense of some of the confusing and some of the repetition in the Book. I now leave my notes as a guide to help you read and discover on your own. I encourage you to write notes over my notes – this exercise will only increase your faith and give you some structure to your study.

Please pray and keep an open mind as you study on your own that God will talk to you.

Mike Stork

"We have come to believe and to know that you are the Holy One of God." John 6:69

Genesis

1. creation: the creation of man let us make man in our image

2. Adam and eve – woman formed from man's rib

3. Fall of man

4. Cain and Abel – anyone who kills Cain will suffer vengeance 7 times over

5. Adam to Noah

6. The flood –

7. Flood continued

8. Flood ends

9. God's covenant with Noah – Noah gets drunk, Ham sees him naked – Curses Ham's descendants – Ham is the father of Canaan

10. Table of nations

11. Tower of Babel – Shem to Abram

12. Abram Sarai; Sarai pretends to be a sister in Egypt

13. Lot goes separate ways;

14. **Abram rescues lot with 317 men: Melchizedek, the priest of the God most high – I WILL ACCEPT NOTHING FROM YOU … SO THAT NO ONE WILL BE ABLE TO SAY 'I MADE ABRAM RICH.'**

15. God makes cov. With Abram

16. Hager gives birth to Ishmael

17. Abram becomes Abraham; Sarai becomes Sarah; Abram laughs at God; starts circumcision

18. Sarah laughs; the lord will spare the city for 50 to 10 people

19. Lot leaves Sodom - cities destroyed- sleeps with daughters

20. Abraham tells someone else Sarah is his sister - this time, God seems fairer

21. Birth of Isaac; Ishmael and Hager sent away

22. God tests Abraham

23. Sarah dies

24. Isaac meets and marries Rebekah

25. Abraham dies; Jacob and Esau born

26. Isaac prospers

27. Jacob gets Isaac's blessing from Esau; then Jacob Flees

28. Jacob's ladder – dream

29. Jacob Marries Leah and Rachel

30. Jacob prospers –

31. Jacob flees unfair father-in-law – Laban

32. Jacob prepares to meet Esau, and he wrestles with God; Jacob becomes Israel

33. Jacob meets Esau

34. Dinah (Jacob's daughter) defiled men circumcised and then killed by her brothers

35. God tells Jacob to move and renames him Israel; Rachel dies giving birth to Israel's 12th son; Isaac Dies

36. Esau's Descendants

37. Joseph Dreams king of Brothers and parents – Joseph sold by bros

38. Onan spills seed so as not to get someone pregnant – God kills him; Judah impregnates his Daughter-in-law; she had posed as a prostitute

39. Joseph and Potiphar's wife; she tries to seduce him

40. Dreams of the Cupbearer and the baker, interpreted by Joseph

41. Pharaoh's Dreams; Joseph in charge of Egypt

42. Joseph's bros go to Egypt – Joseph sends them back for Bro Ben

43. The Bros make a second trip to Egypt

44. The silver cup in Ben's sack

45. Joseph makes himself known

46. Jacob goes to Egypt

47. Pharaoh gives the land of Goshen to Israel; Joseph acquires all of Egypt for Pharaoh

48. Jacob blesses Joseph's sons

49. Jacob blesses his sons

50. Jacob dies Joseph dies

Exodus

1. Israelites oppressed

2. Boys ordered killed

3. birth of Moses; Moses flees Egypt

4. burning bush

5. Moses needs signs. He needs Aaron   Moses almost killed by God

6. pharaoh doubles work

7. god promises deliverance; the family record of Moses

8. Aaron speaks for Moses; plague-blood water

9. plague-frogs; plague-gnats; plague -flies

10. plague-livestock; plague-boils; plague-hail

11. plague-locusts; plague-darkness

12. plague-firstborn

13. Passover exodus

14. 13-14. Consecration of all First Born – Israelites pass through the Red Sea

15. songs of Moses and Miriam water bad- Moses throws wood into it becomes sweet

16. manna; kept some manna in a jar for future generations

17. water water from rock Moses sinned; Moses holds up staff so that Joshua can win a battle

18. Jethro visits Moses and helps set up the judges

19. Mt. Sinai made holy by God

20. 10 commandments

21. 21 laws-Hebrew slaves; personal injuries EYE **FOR EYE NOT REALLY**

22. laws-property social no interest charge virgins

23. HELP **YOUR ENEMIES**; 3 annuals annual feasts Passover harvest ingathering

24. Many see God Moses sprinkles blood on people to confirm cov.

25. making the ark the lamp stand give from the heart

26. making the tabernacle

27. making the alter the courtyard

28. making priest garments-ephod-breast piece

29. consecration of priest - blood sprinkled on priest Aaron and sons

30. incenses $ for atonement rich and poor same $

31. men were chosen to build sacred stuff

32. golden calf - Moses asks God not to wipe out the Israelites - Moses makes people drink gold - Levites volunteer to slaughter 3000 - Moses asks God to take his name out of the book for people Moses said he would take their place and die instead of the Hebrews

33. people take off all ornaments as a sign of repentance - Moses talks face to face to God many times in a tent - Moses sees god's glory backside

34. new stone tablets - Moses asks the lord to let the lord go with us - vs. 14 jealous lord - radiant face of Moses

35. people asked to bring stuff for the Tabernacle

36. people brought more than enough and asked to stop - they worked on it

37. they made -ark-table-lamps-alter

38. they made an alter-wash basin - courtyard - materials used - 603550 men 20 years and older

39. made priest garments - ephod - breast piece - Moses blesses them for Work Done Well

40. set up Tabernacle - God fills tent of meeting and Tabernacle

Leviticus

1. Burnt offering - **INDIVIDUAL TO SLAUGHTER** animal

2. Grain offering

3. Fellowship offering

4. sin offering   slaughter bull goat or sheep

5. various sins poor man's options on what to sacrifice - guilt offering

6. make offering and restitution plus 20 percent Burnt-Grain-Sin offering

7. Guilt offering Fellowship offering made for thankfulness or vow Priests share

8. Ordination of Aaron and sons

9. priests begin ministry. Aaron makes a sacrifice for the people. God consumes the sacrifice

10. Sons of Aaron die by not following orders. Aaron doesn't eat the offering but tells Moses he can't because his kid dies have died

11. Clean and Unclean Food

12. Purification after childbirth

13. Regulations - skin diseases and Mildew

14. cleansing from - skin disease and Mildew

15. Regs. on discharges - semen - monthly periods - women make monthly sacrifices and unclean for weeks every month

16. Day of Atonement - scapegoat to desert and fast

17. Don't eat Blood - Stop sacrificing to goat gods

18. Unlawful sex   - relative - neighbor - man on man

19. Various laws - great commandment - no tattoos

20. Punishment for sin - sex death

21. Rules for priests - High priest must marry a virgin

22. Who can eat the sacrifices - unacceptable sacrifices

23. 6 appointed feasts and Sabbath

24. Lamps to run continually - blasphemer stoned

25. Sabbath year - the year of jubilee

26. Reward and punishments

27. Redeeming stuff that was given to God.

Numbers

1. The Census 603550 men 20-up

   Not counted tribe of Levi

2. Arrangement of camp

3. Levites set aside for priesthood - **REDEEMED FOR ISRAEL FIRSTBORN**

4. Different Levi clan's responsibilities

5. Camp Purity – Restitution for wrongs + one-fifth – test of an unfaithful wife

6. Navi rite What a Nazirite is – the song "the lord blessesbless you and keep you…"

7. Offerings at the dedication of the Tabernacle

8. Setting apart of Levites – they are to take the place of all Israelites that are to be given as firstborn

9. The first Passover feast and what to do if someone is unclean to take it.

10. Trumpets set to signal when to go etc. – They leave Sinai – Moses Father in law goes with them

11. Manna described – complaining, so God gives Quail only to give a severe plague – Moses wants to die, so the responsibility is spread to 70 elders who are filled with the spirit. Moses doesn't think God can feed everyone meat –Joshua appears jealous - belief seems to be in Moses

12. Miriam and Aaron Oppose Moses – **MOSES VERY HUMBLE** – Miriam gets leprosy

13. 12 sent to explore Canaan - Caleb says we can do it

14. People rebel- God tells them they will die in the desert - people then decide to go to Canaan, and arekilled 10 spies are struck down

15. Offerings for various things - Sabbath breaker stoned-must wear tassels

16. Men oppose Moses and Aaron - God swallows them in the ground alive 250 die - group grumbles 14700 die of plague before Aaron can make atonement

17. Aaron staff buds - proof he is the priest

18. The Levites and priest are to get all of the offerings and use them as their wages - they are to give a tenth to the priest

19. RECIPE FOR HOLY WATER

20. Miriam dies - Moses makes water from a rock - Edom denies passage - Aaron dies on a mountain

21. Bronze snake - defeat 4 groups

22. Balaka Balak sends for Balaam - Balaam's donkey talks

23. Balaam 1st 2nd oracle

24. 3rd, 4th, and finale oracle vs. 1, he did not resort to Sorcery vs. 17. A star will come out of Jacob

25. ISRAELITES ISRAELITES HAS RELATIONS WITH MIDIANITE WOMEN AND WORSHIP BAAL - SPEAR DRIVEN THROUGH BOTH

26. 2nd census

27. The daughters get an inheritance - Joshua succeeds Moses

28. Daily offerings – Sabbath – monthly – Passover - Feast of Weeks

29. Feast of trumpets – Day of Atonement – Feast of Tabernacles

30. Vows - by women

31. Killing of Midianites – only virgin women were spared – huge plunder

32. Some tribes decide they like this side of the Jordan – they tell Moses, and he tells them they can have it if they help fight in Canaan

33. List of where they traveled and God's charge to drive everyone out

34. Boundaries of Canaan – cast lots for who gets what – 9 ½ tribes divide it up

35. Cities of refuge, and towns for Levites

36. Daughter's inheritance clarified

Deuteronomy

1. Moses tells of going to take Canaan - repeats the story of - leaders selected - spies sent out - people decide to go without God

2. Wanderings in the desert - do not fight with some. God gave them an inheritance also - defeat Sihon - kill men, women children

3. king struck down - destroy-all people - Moses told again not allowed in Canaan

4. 4.2 do not add or subtract from law 4.29. You will find if you seek

5. 10 commandments

6. 6.4 love the lord - THE GREATEST COMMAND - 6.18 do what is right - 6.24 fear the lord

7. Drive out 7 nations larger than you - but not all at once

8. In the desert, to humble and test - **MAN DOES NOT LIVE BY BREAD ALONE**

9. The land is theirs because the nations now in Canaan are wicked, not because Israel is righteous

10. 10.12 - God wants us to fear - walk in his ways - love him - serve him with heart and soul - observe decrees

11. Love obeys God - teach your children 11.19

12. Rejoice 12.18 don't worship like others worship 12.30- 31

13. **GOD TESTS US 13.3 CLOSE PEOPLE ENTICE YOU; YOU MUST HAVE THEM STONED 13.6**

14. Food - tithes

15. 7 years cancel debts be free with money - free servants on their 7th year

16. 3 celebrations all men must attend -judges

17. Kill people who worship other gods - law courts – rules for the King

18. Levites may move - test prophets - detestable practices

19. Cities of refuge - Witnesses

20. War - officers ask questions before battle - do not destroy fruit trees

21. unsolved murders - marry a captive - the right of the firstborn

22. Various laws - **YOU MUST HELP** - don't wear women's cloths - build a safety net around the house when building - marriage violations - **RAPE IS LIKE MURDER**

23. exclusions from assembly -keep camp clean - slaves - don't become shrine prostitutes - eat in your neighbor's field do not fill the basket

24. divorce - newlyweds stay together 1st year - various laws - kidnapping death - fathers not to be put to death for children

25. Various laws- punishment no more than 40 lashes - duty of brother-in-law - THE FAMILY OF THE UNSADDLED - women do not seize by PRIVATE PARTS - dishonesty

26. First fruits and tithes - did not offer to the dead

27. Set up plaster stones at the Jordan - don'ts

28. Blessings - curses for disobedience - eat own children

29. renewal of covenant - 29.4 **NOT GIVEN YOU A MIND THAT UNDERSTANDS -** 29.19 I will be safe even though I persist in going my own way

30. Prosperity again after returning to God - 30.6 **CIRCUMCISE YOUR HEARTS - 30.10 COMMAND NOT TOO DIFFICULT 30.14 THE WORD IS VERY NEAR YOU** it is in your heart so that you may obey it 30.19 choose life

31. Joshua to succeed Moses - **READ LAW EVERY 7 YEARS** - be strong and courageous - Israel's rebellion predicted

32. Song of Moses

33. Moses blesses the tribes

34. the death of Moses - 34.10 no prophet ever like Moses

Joshua

1. be strong and courageous 3 times

2. Rahab and the spies

3. Crossing the Jordan

4. Israelites circumcised - the day of Passover ate fruit to Canaan - commander of lord's army appears

5. Jericho falls

6. Achan hides plunder - he and his family stoned

7. Ai ambushed - plunder ok -reading of entire law

8. Gibonite deceive Joshua to let them live

9. Sun stands still-hail kills many -5 kings killed - southern cities conquered

10. Northern cities defeated - **JOSHUA TOOK ENTIRE LAND AS COMMANDED**

11. List of defeated kings

12. Division of land

13. Caleb was given land he spied out 45 years earlier -,

14. Caleb gives a daughter to brother - Judah didn't get all the Jebusites from Jerusalem

15. Allotment of 2 more tribes

16. Sisters given land they descended Joseph

17. Cast Lots for the rest of the land,

18. Allotments - Joshua was given a town

19. Cities of refuge set up,

20. Levites given 48 cities – vs. 45 **PROMISES FULFILLED**

21. Eastern tribes return home - make huge alter - almost cause civil war

22. Joshua warns not to fall away

23. Covenant renewed – vs.15 **BUT AS FOR ME AND MY HOUSEHOLD WE WILL SERVE THE LORD** - set up a stone as a witness - Joshua dies

Judges

1. Israel fights remaining Canaanites - cuts a king's toes and thumbs off - Jerusalem burned - descendants of Jethro given land

2. Angel delivers the bad news – Obeyed the Lord throughout Joshua's life and next-generation - **ISRAEL FALLS AWAY - GOD TESTS THEM** VS. 22 NATIONS LEFT BEHIND TO TEST ISRAEL

3. **CALEB'S YOUNGER BROTHER** 1ST JUDGE -   2nd **EHUD** LEFT-HANDED KILLED FAT KING - 3rd **SHAMGAR**

4. **DEBORAH** leads Israel - Jael, a woman, kills the enemy

5. Song of Deborah

6. **GIDEON** called by gods angel - tears down bad alter - asks for a sign from god - dew on wool

7. 32000 men down to 300, defeat Midianites

8. Gideon pursues 2 kings - 300 take 15000 - ephod vs. 27 became bad

9. Wicked Abimelech - son of Gideon - killed Gideon's 70 kids

10-11. **JEPHTHAH** leads Israel - beats ammonites - **IN VOW TO THE LORD SACRIFICES ONLY DAUGHTER**

12. Men of Epkraim – Israelites - go against Jephthah, an Israelite - Jep kills 42000

13. **Sampson** born - to be a Nazarite - angel appears - lord appears in flame - the name of angel beyond understanding

14. Sampson's marriage – a riddle - wife given to a friend

15. Tied up by Israelites - jawbone kills 1000 - God gave a spring to drink

16. Delilah - Samson blinded kills thousands

17. Micah makes his own idols - gets Levite to be his priest

18. Danites take Micah's idols and priest - they attack and take peaceful peoples

19. Levite and his concubine -raped- body cut into 12 parts

20. Israelites kill Benjamites - 50-60000 die in the civil war

21. Wives for 400 surviving Benjamites

Ruth

1. Ruth leaves her land and goes back with Naomi to her land, Judah
2. 2-4 meets and marries Boaz - her kinsman-redeemer
3. Ruth is David's grandmother

1 Samuel

1. Hannah gives birth and dedicates Samuel to God - **PRAYS WITH HEART**

2. Hannah song - Eli the high priest at Shiloh - Eli's sons wicked - prophecy against house of Eli

3. Samuel thought Eli was calling him - 3 times he heard his name, and he would run to Eli and say Here am I - vs. 7 did not know God or word - vs19 let none of his words fall to the ground

4. Philistines kill 30000 Israelites - Eli dies 2 sons die, Daughter-in-law dies - **CAPTURE THE ARK**

5. Philistines move ark from city to city because it brings death and boils

6. Ark returned with 5 gold rats and 5 gold boils - sent back by 2 cows - 70 Israelites killed for looking in the ark

7. Samuel tells Israel to get rid of all other gods - they do - he asks god to help, and god causes thunder, and they route the enemy

8. **ISRAEL ASKS FOR A KING - VS. 7 NOT YOU. THEY HAVE REJECTED, BUT THEY HAVE REJECTED ME-GOD-AS, THEIR KING**

9. Saul from smallest clan smallest tribe of Israel - head taller than anyone

10. Samuel anoints Saul - prophesied - vs. 9 gods changed Saul's heart - Saul declared king - valiant men's hearts touched by god

11. Saul rescues the city of Jabesh - Saul reaffirmed as king

12. Samuel's farewell speech - evil to ask for the a king - vs. 20 you have done... Evil, yet do not turn...Lord - vs. 24 serve.... with all your heart

13. Saul acts like a high priest - Sam tells him that because of another bloodline to become king-no swords in all of Israel – battle with axes, goads, plows, etc.

14. Jonathon attacks Phil. kills 20- Israel then routes Phil. with God - John. Eats Honey - John to die - rescued by men

15. vs. 22 **DOES THE LORD DELIGHT IN BURNT OFFERINGS...AS MUCH AS IN OBEYING** - Saul attacks but takes plunder - Sam. sees Saul for the last time

16. Sam. anoints David - David becomes Saul's armor bearer and musician

17. David and Goliath

18. Saul Jealous of David - Saul tries to kill him - Saul gives his daughter to David - Jonathon loves David

19. Saul tries to kill David - spears again - David's wife helps him flee

20. David and Jonathon - Jon. Warns David - Saul hurls at spear at Jon.

21. David flees - goes to the temple, given bread and Goliath's sword - **ACTS LIKE A MADMAN IN FRONT OF A KING OF GATH**

22. David hides his mom and Dad with the king of Moab- Saul kills' priest family town men, women children

23. David and 600 men save a town. - Saul almost catches David

24. David spares Saul's life - he cuts part of his robe

25. Samuel dies - David almost kills Nabal - Abigail persuades him not to - Nabal dies of stroke - David marries Abigal and another - Saul gives David's wife Michal to someone else

26. David spares Saul again - takes spear and jug

27. David lives among Philistines - becomes a raider

28. Witch of Endor makes contact with Samuel for Saul

29. **KING OF PHILISTINES HAS TO TELL DAVID THAT HE CAN'T FIGHT AGAINST ISRAEL**

30. Ziklag is destroyed - David's wives are taken, and his men want to stone him - God helps him rescue everyone and everything

31. Saul commits suicide - Jonathon and brothers die - Philistines display bodies and armor - valiant men take down bodies

2 Samuel

1. David learns of Saul's death - kills the messenger - mourns for Jon. and Saul

2. David anointed king of Judah - Ish-Bosheth, son of Saul, became king of Israel - David's house and Saul's house begin a long fight

3. Abner, mad at the king of Israel, goes to all the tribes and gets them to agree to make David king - Abner visits David and is murdered to avenge a brother - David is upset

4. Ish Bosheth - king of Israel - murdered - again, messengers tell David, and he kills them

5. David - at 30 - becomes king - serves 33 years - 7 years as king of Judah - 40 years - Defeats Phil. and Jerusalem - City of David

6. **DAVID BRINGS ARK TO JERUSALEM- UZZAH TOUCHES ARK AND DIES - DAVID SCARED OF GOD AND ARK**

7. David wants to make a house for God - God tells him about his offspring - Jesus - vs. 12 - will be forever

8. David defeats many nations - Moabites are measured, and every 3rd killed

9. David restores Jonathan's son as one of his sons - Mephibosheth

10. Army defeats large army after Delegation humiliated - beards and clothes cut

11. David and Bathsheba - 2 times Uriah refuses to sleep with his wife

12. Nathan rebukes David - the story of lamb - son die - vs13 sinned - Solomon born

13. Amnon rapes Tamar - Absalom kills Amnon and flees

14. Absalom returns to Jerusalem - he is very handsome with thick hair

15. Absalom's conspiracy - Ab. Declares himself king - David flees

16. Ziba tells David about Saul's grandson David gives land to Ziba - Shimei curses David

17. 16-17. Hushai and Ahithophel give Absalom advice - H., loyal to David, gives bad advice - A. gives good advice - when not taken, kills himself

18. Absalom's hair tangles in a tree - men slay him.

19. David mourns. David returns to Jerusalem - forgives Shimei and Saul's grandson

20. Sheba rebels against David - a wise woman has his head cut off and given to Joab

21. Gibeonite's avenged - 7 of Saul's descendants sacrificed to stop Drought - spared Jon. Son - war with Philistines Goliaths relatives killed including brother and 6-fingered man

22. David's song of Praise - the lord is my rock - vs. 24 I have been blameless

23. David s mighty men - 37 in all, including Uriah - mixed bread -3 more famous than all

24. David counts the fighting men - the Lord incites David -3 choices - 3 days of plague - David sees angel - vs. 24 buys threshing floor

1 Kings

1. Adonijah sets himself as king- David makes Solomon king

2. David's charge to Solomon - advice forgiveness and revenge - Solomon does as David says - shows great respect for Mother

3. Solomon asks for wisdom – God pleased – two women fight over baby

4. List of Solomon's Officials – Daily provisions listed – Wisdom, spoke 3000 proverbs, 1005 songs, taught on plants and animals

5. Solomon starts building the temple – 30,000 were sent to another land to start work

6. Solomon Builds the temple – no hammers for stone at the building site – overlaid everything with pure gold in parts of the temple – 7 years to build

7. Solomon builds his Palace – 13 years to build – List of temple furnishings

8. Ark brought to the temple – God's cloud filled the temple – Solomon's prayer of dedication – VS 27 the heavens cannot contain you (God).... vs. 46 there is no one who does not sin. - Prayed on knees with hands stretched to the sky

9. Lord appears to Solomon and warns him to stay faithful – Pharaoh attacks Gezer and gives him as a wedding present

10. Queen of Sheba – overwhelmed by Solomon's splendor – so rich silver became common as rocks

11. **SOLOMON'S WIVES TURN HIM TO OTHER GODS** - the Lord raised up adversaries to Solomon. – one fled as a boy to Egypt and married Pharaoh's sister, children raised with Pharaoh's children – **JEROBOAM TOLD BY A PROPHET THAT HE WILL RULE 10 TRIBES OF ISRAEL** VS 39 humble David's descendants … but not forever. – Solomon dies – ruled for 40 years.

12. Rehoboam becomes king of Judah - Jeroboam becomes king of Israel, sets up golden calves

13. The man of God from Judah warns Jeroboam that human bones will be offered on the Altar – **THE KING's HAND SHRIVELED UP –**

THE PROPHET HEALED THE KING – PROPHET KILLED BY LION ON THE WAY HOME

14. Ahijah's Prophecy against king Jeroboam – Boy dies minute mother steps foot in the house – vs. 9 Jeroboam did more evil than all before, therefore, all descendants to be wiped out – Rehoboam becomes king of Judah – also wicked

15. Abijah became king of Judah – wicked – vs. 5 only sins listed of David was Uriah's case – **Asa** King of Judah – good king – even removed grandmother for worshipping other Gods – **NADAB** king of Judah killed Jeroboam's whole family – Baasha King of Israel – he did evil

16. Baasha told his house will go like Jeroboam – Elah, king of Israel – is killed while drunk – Zimri becomes king and kills all of Baasha's family and friends – Zimri becomes king –the city he is in is attacked, and he sets fire to the palace and dies – Israel has two factions for new king Omri defeats Tibni – Ahab becomes the most sinful king of Israel – worships Baal in a temple he built

17. **ELIJAH TELLS AHAB THAT IT WILL NOT RAIN** – flees and is fed by Ravens – water dries up, goes to the widow's house, then eats from the never-ending flour and oil – raises the Widow's son from death

18. Elijah and Obadiah – apparently Ahab had been trying to find Elijah to kill him – Elijah presents himself to the king and tells everyone to assemble at Mt Carmel – Elijah calls down fire and consumes the altar - kills 850 of Baal & Asherah – Out runs the kings Chariot

19. Jezebel is mad at Elijah and threatens him – he flees and wants to die – The Lord appears to Elijah – anoints Elisha – told to anoint two new kings, one for Israel and one for Aram

20. Ben-Hadad attacks Ahab – takes family, gold, and silver – wants more, Ahab refuses – Ahab defeats Ben-Hadad – Ahab makes a treaty with Ben-Hadad – **BECAUSE OF TREATY** AHAB IS CONDEMNED TO DIE BY A PROPHET

21. **Jezebel has Naboth stoned** so Ahab could take his Vineyard – Elijah condemns Ahab (like Jeroboam and Baasha) Vs. 25 never a man like Ahab who sold himself to evil – **AHAB HUMBLES HIMSELF SO GOD PULLS BACK ON HIS PUNISHMENT VS. 29**

22. Micaiah lies to Ahab and then tells the truth about the upcoming battle – explains that God sent a spirit to lie to the prophets – Ahab is killed as prophesized – **JEHOSHAPHAT** GOOD KING of Judah – Son of Ahab, Ahaziah Bad, king of Israel

2 Kings

1. King Ahaziah falls and breaks his legs – Elijah tells him he will die there after 50 men come, and he burns them up – twice

2. Elijah is taken up to heaven – Parts the Jordon with cloak – Elisha gets a double portion of spirit – also parts water – Heals water – youths call him bald head – they are killed

3. Moab revolts – Jehoshaphat goes with kings to defeat them – Elisha tells them they will succeed

4. Elisha – Widow's oil – Shunammite told of the birth of a son and raised from dead – Death in the pot – **FEEDING OF 100**

5. Elisha – Naaman healed of leprosy dips 7 times in Jordon – **SERVANT GEHAZI GETS LEPROSY FOR TAKING MONEY**

6. Elisha – Ax head floats – **SURROUNDED BY TROOPS HE OPENS THE EYES OF SERVANT TO SEE GOD'S ARMY OUTNUMBERED THE ATTACKERS** – captures them and releases them

7. Elisha = city of Samaria besieged – then God causes noise to sound like an army and other army fled – **MAN THAT DOUBTED THE PROPHECY WAS TRAMPLED TO DEATH JUST AS FORESEEN**

8. The woman (Shunammite)'s land was restored – Hazael Murders king Ben-Hadad – Jehoram and Ahaziah, Kings of Judah – both married into Ahab's family and sinned.

9. **JEHU** anointed king by the prophet of Elisha – Jehu was a commander in the army – Jehu Kills king Joram, King Ahaziah, and Jezebel – Jezebel is thrown down and splattered

10. **JEHU,** KING OF ISRAEL, KILLS ALL RELATED TO AHAB – **KILLS ALL MINISTERS OF BAAL – DESTROYS BAAL'S TEMPLE AND ROCK – USED AS LATRINE**

11. mother of Ahaziah, Athaliah - kills all the royal family - **JOASH** HIDDEN - TAKES THROWN AT 7 YEARS OLD

12. **Joash** repairs temple - Joash gives all gold items dedicated in the temple to another king to stop the war

13. Jehoahaz king of Israel – Jehoash King of Israel – Elisha tells the king to shoot arrows – Elisha dies – man thrown into Elisha's tomb touches bones COMES BACK TO LIFE – VS 21

14. Amaziah, king of Judah, became too bold and was captured by Israel – Jeroboam II, king of Israel – even though badblessed because of promises to Israel

15. **AZARIAH** King of Judah – Leper king – Zechariah King of Israel reigned 6 months – Shallum King of Israel reigned one month – Pekahiah king of Israel – Pekah king of Israel (killed Pekahiah) – **JOTHAM** KING OF JUDAH GOOD KING

16. Ahaz, king of Judah – did evil – sacrificed his son – redid the altar, and changed a lot of the temple stuff – to please the King of Assyria

17. **HOSHEA LAST KING OF ISRAEL** – captured by Assyria people deported – Exiled because of sin – **VS. 14 DID NOT TRUST IN THE LORD – VS 15 FOLLOWED WORTHLESS IDOLS AND BECAME WORTHLESS THEMSELVES** – Samaria resettled with all sorts of people

18. **KING HEZEKIAH** – King of Judah while Israel was taken into captivity – very good King – OBEYED GOD – TORE DOWN OTHER GODS EVEN BRONZE SNAKE OF MOSES – Stands up to Syria

19. **ISAIAH TELLS THE KING NOT TO WORRY BUT HOLD FAST – HEZEKIAH'S PRAYER – AN ANGEL OF GOD PUT TO DEATH 185,000 ASSYRIANS WHILE THEY WERE ASLEEP – KING OF ASSYRIA, SENNACHERIB KILLED** by his own sons while worshipping Nisroch

20. Hezekiah's illness – **GOD ADDED 15 YEARS TO HIS LIFE** – made the shadow go backward – envoys from Babylon – Isaiah says that Judah will end up in Babylon

21. Manasseh, King of Judah – very wicked, rebuilt high places – sacrificed his own son – shed innocent blood all over Jerusalem – Amon, king of Judah, also evil – assassinated, then the people killed the assassins

22. **THE BOOK OF LAW FOUND WHILE REMODELING THE TEMPLE – KING JOSIAH** tore his robes and repented – vs. 19 because you humbled yourself... will not see the disaster of Judah

23. **JOSIAH RENEWS LAW DESTROYS FOREIGN GODS AND TEMPLES – BURNS HUMAN BONES ON THEIR ALTARS AS PROPHESIZED** – Josiah killed by Pharaoh

24. **Jehoiakim** King of Judah – captured by Nebuchadnezzar, king of Babylon – everyone was taken into captivity except the poorest people vs. 14 - Zedekiah made King of Judah by Nebuchadnezzar

25. Fall of Jerusalem – King Zedekiah rebelled against Babylon – they took everything from the temple – burned all the buildings and broke the wall – had priests and officials killed – killed the king's kids and put the king's eyes out – Babylon appointed another to be Governor he was assassinated by royal line – KING **JEHOIACHIM** RELEASED FROM BABYLON PRISON

I Chronicles

1. Birth records – Adam to Noah – Abraham – Isaac – Rulers of Edom before Israel

2. Israel's sons – then concentrates on Judah and gives the record of Judah and Caleb – Caleb who? Vs. 8 Ethan

3. Sons of David – Kings of Judah – **ROYAL LINE AFTER EXILE**

4. Other clans of Judah – **PRAYER OF JABEZ** to expand territory and free from pain – genealogy of Simeon

5. Genealogy of Reuben – Gad – ½ tribe of Manasseh – Reuben lost birthright although Judah was stronger than Joseph – **VS. 20 HE ANSWERED THEIR PRAYERS BECAUSE THEY TRUSTED HIM** – vs. 25 famous but disobeyed God

6. Levi

7. Issachar - Benjamin - Naphtali - Manasseh - Ephraim - Ashser

8. Benjamites - Saul - **DIVORCE VS. 8**

9. People in Jerusalem after the exile – **VERY FEW NUMBERS IN THE THOUSANDS** – vs. 31 bread for every Sabbath – Genealogy of Saul

10. Saul takes his life – **vs. 13 Saul died because … unfaithful…. Etc.**

11. David Becomes king – David conquers Jerusalem – Joab becomes commander in chief – David's Mighty Men

12. Warriors join King David – all the tribes came together to make David King of Israel – vs. 40 joy in Israel

13. The Ark is brought back, and there is much celebrating – Uzzah reaches out to steady it and dies – **DAVID, MAD AND AFRAID, LEAVES THE ARK FOR 3 MONTHS WITH A FAMILY**

14. David's house was built by another King as a gift – David defeats the Philistines – burns their Gods

15. **ARK BROUGHT TO JERUSALEM – THIS TIME BROUGHT ON POLES AS MOSES HAD INSTRUCTED, NOT ON AN OX CART** – David added musical instruments and danced as he entered the city – David's wife despised him for his actions

16. David's psalm of thanks – vs. 26 gods are idols, but the lord made the heavens – vs. 41 … 'for his loves endures forever.' Vs. 36 people said amen and praised the lord

17. God's promise to David – David wants to build a house for God instead of a tent – God seems pleased and tells David that he will make his house – tells of one to come that he will be God's son – David prays – vs. 17 you have spoken of the future – vs. 23 let the promise you made be established forever **VS. 25 FOUND COURAGE TO PRAY TO YOU.**

18. David's victories - repeat

19. Battle against Amorites - repeat

20. Capture of Rabbah - war with philistines - repeat

21. David numbers fighting men - repeat - after bringing Ark to Jerusalem

22. David prepares to build the temple -orders everyone to help Solomon

23. Levites counted – David gives instructions on how they are to work since they wouldn't have to move the tabernacle anymore – instructions to musicians

24. Division of Priest – cast lots in front of David

25. Singers and prophets accompanied by harps, lyres, and cymbals – cast lots

26. The gatekeepers – treasurers – judges – king's servants – Moses's descendant is a treasurer

27. Army divisions – officers of tribes – king's overseers – **HUSHAI WAS THE KING'S FRIEND**

28. God has given David plans for the temple – he is giving instructions to Solomon and the people VS 4 king of Israel forever vs. 9 **GOD KNOWS OUR EVERY MOTIVE** – vs. 12 and 19 God gave plans to David

29. David tells of all the gold, silver, etc., he has set aside for the temple – he pledges his personal fortune to the temple – they assemble then gives freely and wholeheartedly to the lord – David praises God Vs. 14 Everything from God – vs. **GOD TESTS THE HEART** – Death of David

2 Chronicles

1. Solomon asks for wisdom – repeat

2. Solomon starts building the temple and his house – repeat – forces aliens to do labor

3. Solomon **BUILDS THE TEMPLE ON THE VERY SPOT THAT DAVID TALKED TO THE LORD ON THE THRESHING FLOOR.**

4. Solomon has the furnishings done. The Sea was for the priest to wash

5. The Ark is brought to the temple – repeat – many sacrifices couldn't be counted – God comes in a cloud

6. Solomon prays and dedicates the temple – **PRAY TOWARD TEMPLE** and God answers from heaven – **FOREIGNER PRAYS TOWARD TEMPLE** and God answers - Oath in front of temple binding

7. Solomon finished praying, fire came down and consumed the offering – people saw and worshiped – vs. 13 when I shut the heavens or send locusts, etc.

8. Solomon conscripted for his slave labor force

9. Repeat - Queen of Sheba Solomon's splendor

10. **REHOBOAM REJECTS OLD MEN'S ADVICE** - forced labor chief stoned - **JUDAH SPLIT FROM ISRAEL**

11. **<u>REHOBOAM TAKES JUDAH AND BENJAMIN - PRIESTS AND LEVITES COME BECAUSE JEROBOAM REJECTED THEM, AND THEY SET UP THEIR OWN PRIESTS FOR THEIR IDOLS</u>**

12. Rehoboam abandons the law - repents - evil again

13. Abijah, king of Judah, defeats 800000 Israelites, and Jeroboam vs. 18 relied on the lord

14. Asa king of Judah good -**vs. 11 POWERLESS...HELP US.... WE RELY ON YOU**

15. Asa reforms Judah - **ISRAELITES COME TO JUDAH BECAUSE THEY WORSHIP GOD** - vs. 2 and **15 SEEK ... FIND** - tore down grandmas Asherah pole

16. **ISRAEL'S KING TRIES TO BUILD WALLS TO KEEP PEOPLE FROM GOING TO JUDAH** - Asa gets another king to beat up Israel god says since you didn't rely on God, you will be at war - vs. 12 **WHEN SICK RELIED ONLY ON DOCTORS NOT THE LORD**

17. **JEHOSHAPHAT** king of Judah - sent out officials and priests to teach from the book of the law - became very wealthy - all Judah turned and feared God

18. Repeat - Micaiah prophesies against Ahab - God sends a lying spirit vs. 21 Ahab dies vs. 31 **JEHOSHAPHAT CRIES OUT, AND THE LORD HELPS HIM**

19. Jehoshaphat appoints judges - vs. 2 should you help the wicked

20. great army comes to fight Judah. They seek God - a Levite is filled with the spirit and tells them were to go to win - they go and find only dead bodies - takes 3 days to collect plunder - Jehoshaphat makes an alliance with Israel and reprimanded for not relying on God

21. Jehoram, son of Jehoshaphat, becomes king of Judah – **KILLS HIS BROTHERS – PUNISHED WITH A DISEASE WERE HIS BOWELS** come out – died – no one regret and not buried with other kings

22. Ahaziah, son of Jehoram, lasted a year – went to see the son of Ahab, who was wounded and killed by Jehu, who was destroying the house of Ahab. Grandmother went to kill the royal family of Ahaziah, but Joash survived by hiding

23. Jehoiada, the priest, makes Joash the king and kills Grandmother Athaliah

24. Joash, king of Judah, was good as long as Jehoiada the priest was alive - they restored the temple - once the priest died, the king had the son of the priest stoned and brothers killed - King Joash was wounded in battle and killed in his bed

25. Amaziah king of Judah - prophet tells king don't take hired Israelites to battle - vs. **9 WHAT ABOUT SILVER VS. 10 GOD WILL**

GIVE YOU MORE - slaughter 10,000 by throwing off the cliff - takes idols and worships - is killed

26. **UZZIAH** king of Judah – **GOOD UNTIL HE BECAME FULL OF PRIDE** – Developed machines to hurl stones – went into the temple to burn incense, priest confronted him, and he broke out in leprosy – had leprosy until he died and lived in separate palace buried by kings but not with kings

27. **JOTHAM,** king of Judah – vs. 6, grew powerful because he walked steadfastly…

28. Ahaz – king of Judah – wicked – **SACRIFICED HIS SONS** – Israel defeated Judah and took 200000 people – Prophet Oded told them they shouldn't take their brothers captive – Israel clothed them and let go – King **AHAZ STARTED WORSHIPING OTHER GODS BECAUSE THEY DEFEATED HIM** – closed the temple – set up alters on every corner.

29. **HEZEKIAH** purifies the temple – service of the temple reestablished the first month of his kingdom

30. Hezekiah celebrates the Passover – sends couriers that were ridiculed – people came but weren't purified according to the law. – King prayed that they would be pardoned vs. 18-20 – everyone stayed a week longer vs. 27 God heard them

31. Tithes reestablished, and everyone gives generously – priest and Levites have plenty and some left over – vs. 21 **… HE SOUGHT HIS GOD AND WORKED WHOLEHEARTEDLY. AND SO, HE PROSPERED.**

32. King of Assyria threatens Judah – Hezekiah says to be strong and courageous. We have a greater power vs. 7 – an angel of God strikes down the Assyrians – vs. 27 Hezekiah very rich – vs. 31 God left him to test him when the Babylonians came to know everything in his heart

33. Manasseh, king of Judah, did evil – sacrificed sons, built alter and poles to other gods – taken to Babylon by a ring in his nose – repented and came back to Jerusalem – Amon, King of Judah – evil – killed by his own men

34. **JOSIAH** reforms the remnant – the book is found and read from – **JOSIAH REPENTS AND PUTS OFF DISASTER FOR A GENERATION**

35. Josiah prepares the Passover – the best one since the time of Samuel – Dies in battle – was told by another king that God had told him to do this, so don't oppose me vs. 22

36. Kings of Judah – Jehoahaz, Jehoiakim, Jehoiachin, Zedekiah – vs. **16 LORD SENT MANY TO MESSENGERS, BUT THE PEOPLE MOCKED THEM** – Jerusalem falls – temple burned – Cyrus king of Persia rebuilds the temple.

Ezra

1. Cyrus, king of Persia - helps exiles return

2. List of exiles who returned

3. Rebuilding the temple and altar - us. 12 **MANY WEPT BECAUSE IT WAS SMALLER** foundation - **MANY JOYFUL**

4. People offer to help rebuild and are told no must be done by Israelites - told to stop by another king

5. **HAGGAI** AND **ZECHARIAH** tell them to rebuild anyway - Tattenai complains to the king of Assyria Darius

6. Darius finds a memo from King Cyrus telling him to rebuild and pray for him - completion and dedication of the temple - Jews celebrate Passover

7. Ezra was a descendant of Aaron and could be a high priest - the king tells Ezra to return with gold and, people, and temple stuff - speaks in first person vs. 22.

8. List of family heads returning with Ezra – vs.22 ASHAMED **TO ASK KING FOR GUARDS TO HELP THEM BACK TO JUDAH AFTER STATING THAT GOD WAS WITH THEM, SO THEY FASTED TO ASK FOR GOD'S HELP**

9. Ezra learns of the intermarriage of the people – is appalled – tears tunic – prays and fasts – holy race vs. 2

10. People confess sin and get rid of foreign wives and children

Nehemiah

1. Nehemiah – saddened by learning that the walls and gates to Jerusalem were down = prayed to God, confessing his sins and the sins of the Israelites – He was a cupbearer to the king

2. The king grants Nehemiah's request to rebuild – He goes there with a small army of the king –inspects the wall at night then announces what he is doing

3. List of builders of the wall and where they rebuilt

4. Opposition to the rebuilding – Nehemiah ended up putting out guards – ½ to work ½ to guard. also, they slept in their clothes so as to be ready for attack and carried swords everywhere

5. Jews were getting usury from fellow Jews to the point that they had to sell their daughters – Nehemiah – very angry vs. 6 – appointed gov. of Judah – didn't take any food or land but devoted himself to the rebuilding

6. Plots against Nehemiah meet on the plain of Ono to kill him. **ENEMY PAID A PROPHET TO INTIMIDATE HIM** – wall completed in 52 days. Nobles kept in touch with Nehemiah's enemies

7. Nehemiah puts his brother in charge of Jerusalem and Hananiah because of his integrity and because he feared God vs. 2 – list of returnees same as Ezra 2

8. Ezra reads the law, and the others instruct the people – first, the people weep, then they understand the word and are full of joy – celebrate the feast of tabernacles (booths)

9. The Israelites read the book for ¼ of the day and confess and worship for ¼ of the day–long prayer reviewing how they got here and that they are now slaves to foreign kings vs. 17 God slow to anger, gracious…. Vs. 28 As soon as at rest, started sinning (part of prayer)

10. Agreement of the people with God – restate some laws – not to intermarry – no buying on the Sabbath – 1/3 shekel to the temple every year – Levites to bring wood every month to the temple – reinstate tithes and dedication of the firstborn

11. New residents I Jerusalem – cast lots so 1 in 10 families would stay in Jerusalem. Some volunteered – people listed

12. priests and Levites listed who stayed in Jerusalem – dedication of the wall – Lots of choirs and musical instruments and joy heard far away

13. final reforms – told to exclude all of the foreign descent – Kicked Tobiah out of the storeroom – made sure portions given to singers and Levites – stopped selling of food on the Sabbath – pulled a man by his hair for intermarriage – vs. 26 even Solomon led astray by women

Esther

1. Queen Vashti deposed

2. Esther is chosen and made queen – Mordecai foils a plot to kill the king

3. Mordecai refuses to give honor to Haman – Harman plots to kill Mordecai and all Jews

4. Mordecai persuades Esther to help – key vs. of book – vs. 12-16 **YOU ARE HERE FOR A PURPOSE** – someone else will rise to help if you don't

5. Esther goes to the king and risks death – she invites the King and Haman to a dinner – Haman sees Mordecai and hates him more friends convince him to build high gallows vs. 9 Mordecai showed no fear

6. Mordecai was honored by the king – Haman stated a way to honor (he thought it was for him) and ended up for Mordecai

7. Haman was Hanged on gallows built for Mordecai –

8. King's edict written by Mordecai – allowed the Jews to protect themselves – Many foreigners became Jews because fear had seized them vs. 17

9. Jews ended up killing their enemies – 75,000 in all – all in one day – started celebrating Purim in the last month on the 14th and 15th (giving presents to each other)

10. Greatness of Mordecai

Job

1. Job greatest man among people of the east – Satan wipes out stuff and children

2. Satan inflicts Job with boils – 3 friends show up and don't speak for 7 days

3. Job speaks – depressed wishes never born – life meaningless – vs. 26 no peace no quietness

4. Eliphaz – those who plow evil sow evil – at the breath of God destroyed – vs. 18 if he charges angels with errors

5. vs. 7 man is born to trouble – God will rescue from calamities

6. Job – vs. 21, you have proved no help vs. 24, show me where I am wrong vs. 28, would I lie to your face

7. still depressed nightmares, can't sleep – skin is clothed in worms and scabs vs. 18 TEST HIM EVERY MOMENT vs.21 why do you not pardon my offenses

8. Bildad – your children sinned and died – vs. 14 what he trusts in is fragile, spider's web vs. 20-22 God rejects evildoers and strengthens a blameless man

9. Job – vs. 2 how can a mortal be righteous before God – vs. 10-11 he performs many miracles, and I can't see him when he passes me vs. 24 If it is not, he, then who is it?

10. Job – I loathe my life – vs. 12 you gave me life and watched over my spirit vs. 15 guilty woes to me if innocent can't hold my help up from shame

11. Zophar - be patient - this trouble will be over, and you will hardly remember - vs. 6. God has forgotten some of your sins vs. 16

12. God makes everything happen - vs. 3 I am not inferior to you

13. Job wants to argue with God face to face

14. Job takes about death and resurrection

15. Eliphaz --vs. 20 all his days, the wicked man suffers

16. 16-17. Job - miserable comforters vs. 16.20 my intercessor to God vs. 17.14 if I claim sin, where is my hope

17. Bildad – vs. are we cattle – stupid in your sight vs. 21 surely such is the dwelling of an evil man

18. Job – How long will you torment me – if I have gone astray, my error remains my concern – everyone has deserted me – even little boys mock me – vs. 20 skin of my teeth – vs. 25 **I KNOW THAT MY REDEEMER LIVES**

19. Zophar – evil gets bad things – vs. 18 he will not enjoy the profit from his trading

20. Job – Evil men prosper – no calamity to them- vs. 19 God stores up a man's punishment for his sons – what does he care

21. Eliphaz – Can a man benefit God? Vs.2 – you are wicked, so repent – God will restore you

22. I want to argue with God – I have not departed from his commands vs. 12 - vs. 15 I am terrified before him

23. Men sin, kill, steal, and yet God charges no one with wrongdoing vs. 12

24. Bildad – How can a man be righteous before God? Vs. 4

25. Job – about the power of God – vs. 7 **HE SUSPENDS THE EARTH OVER NOTHING – VS. 8 CLOUDS ARE WATER**

26. Fate god allows wicked - their offspring will suffer

27. Precious stones are made by fire deep in the ground vs. 5 . but where can wisdom be found vs. 13 it can't be found in the land of living - **vs. 28 WISDOM - FEAR OF LORD - SHUN EVIL IS UNDERSTANDING**

28. . Job remembers his blessings of the past

29. But now they mock me -

30. vs. 1 not to look lustfully - we all come from the womb and are equal vs. 15 - I could do no wrong for fear vs. 23 - sins trust in fortune rejoice in enemies' misfortune - concealing sin bad vs. 33.

31. **ELIHU - 4TH MAN SPEAKS - SPIRIT IN A MAN - BREATH OF GOD THAT GIVES UNDERSTANDING VS. 8 - VS. 18 SPIRIT WITHIN COMPELS ME**

32. VS. 14 HOW GOD SPEAKS - HE SAVES US OVER AND OVER VS. 27-30

33. Elihu - vs. 10. God can do no evil - vs. -14 he withdraws his spirit mankind would perish- vs. 31-33 if l has done wrong I will not do it again should God reward on your terms

34. vs. 5-8 how does your sin or righteousness affect him - if only affects you

35. vs.10-11 repent and prosper - vs. 16. He is wooing you from the jaws of distress - vs. 21 you seem to turn to evil than prefer affliction - vs.33 even the cattle know when a storm approach

36. He controls the weather as a reward and punishment

37. The lord speaks - do you know the laws of the heavens vs. 33 - who provides food for the animals

38. Animals as examples - vs. 13 storks

39. Hippo

40. Crocodile

41. vs. 6 repent for being over righteous (my interpretation) - restored

Psalms

Book 1

1. Blessed is the man who delights in the law

2. The anointed one - kiss the son

3. HELP - I will not fear 10000 - deliver me

4. **MEN LOVE DELUSIONS AND FALSE GODS**- in anger do not sin - trust in god

5. In the morning, I pray and lay out my requests, and wait in expectation

6. Do not rebuke me in your anger – HELP me in my sickness

7. I take refuge in you – vs. 4 without cause have robbed my foe

8. O lord, our Lord, how majestic is your name – vs. 5. Made man a little lower than angels, but everything under our feet

9. My enemies turn back – strike them with terror – let them know they are men

10. Pride the wicked does not seek him – His (wicked prideful man) ways are always prosperous – he is evil

11. In the lord, I will take refuge

12. The wicked freely strut about when the vile is honored among them Vs. 8

13. How long – will you forget me? But I trust in the Lord

14. **FOOL SAYS IN HIS HEART THERE IS NO GOD**

15. **KEEPS OATH EVEN WHEN IT HURTS** – he who does these things will never be shaken

16. Even at night, my heart instructs me – vs.10 **NOR WILL YOU LET THE HOLY ONE SEE DECAY.**

17. Probe and test my heart – then save me

18. **I LOVE YOU, O LORD** - with my God, I can scale a wall – The Lord lives. Praise be my rock!

19. The law of the Lord is perfect, reviving the soul – Vs. 12 Forgive my hidden faults, **KEEP YOUR SERVANT ALSO FROM WILLFUL SINS; MAY THEY NOT RULE OVER ME.**

20. May he give you the desire of your heart and make all your plans succeed.

21. O Lord, the king rejoices in your strength.

22. **JESUS ON THE CROSS**

23. **THE LORD IS MY SHEPHERD** –

24. **THE EARTH IS THE LORD's AND EVERYTHING IN IT**

25. Do not let me be put to shame

26. I have led a blameless life - test me

27. The lord, my light and my salvation - I will sing and make music - day of trouble

28. Those who speak cordially – but harbor malice

29. The voice of the Lord is….

30. **HIS ANGER LASTS A MOMENT, BUT HIS FAVOR LASTS A LIFETIME**

31. I hate those who cling to idols – I trust in you, O Lord – My times are in your hands – In my alarm, I said, "I am cut off from your sight!"

32. Blessed is he whose transgressions are forgiven, whose sins are covered. Blessed is the man whose sin the Lord does not count against him - I will confess … AND **YOU FORGAVE THE GUILT OF MY SIN.**

33. Music instruments – he watches all who live on earth – **NO KING IS SAVED BY HIS ARMY** – no warrior escapes by his strength, a horse is vain to hope for deliverance – But the eyes of the lord are on all who fear him

34. **A RIGHTEOUS MAN MAY HAVE MANY TROUBLES, BUT THE LORD DELIVERS HIM FROM THEM ALL VS. 19**

35. Say to my soul, you are my salvation – the angel of the Lord driving them away – humbled myself with fasting

36. The wicked are like this

37. ***** DO NOT FRET – TRUST IN THE LORD – COMMIT – BE STILL – REFRAIN FROM ANGER – MEEK INHERIT THE LAND AND ENJOY GREAT PEACE - THE WICKED BORROW AND DO NOT REPAY – I HAVE NEVER SEEN THE RIGHTEOUS FORSAKEN OR THEIR CHILDREN BEGGING**

38. Because of my sin, my guilt has overwhelmed me – I am filled with pain – I confess my iniquity. I am troubled by my sin – do not forsake me

39. My life is but a breath – My hope is in you to save me from my transgressions

40. **BLESSED IS THE MAN THAT TRUSTS IN THE LORD – YOU DON'T WANT SACRIFICE – YOU DESIRE ME TO DO YOUR WILL** – troubles surround me, my sins have overtaken me

41. Blesses is he who has regard for the weak

Book II

42. As the Deer pants… - why are you downcast, my soul, put your hope in God

43. why are you downcast, my soul? Put your hope in God

44. By you, we won –, but now you have rejected us – Awake – Rouse yourself!

45. the King and princess are great – your memory will be forever

46. God is an ever-present help in trouble – his voice melts the earth

47. Praise to God – how awesome is the Lord

48. How great Zion is – (Jerusalem)

49. why should I fear evildoers – those who trust in their wealth – **DO NOT BE OVERAWED WHEN A MAN GROWS RICH –**

50. **VS. 15 CALLS UPON ME IN THE DAY OF TROUBLE; I WILL DELIVER YOU, AND YOU WILL HONOR ME. -- GOD DOESN'T NEED SACRIFICES OR TO EAT**

51. Psalm of repentance – David after Nathan confronted him – vs. 10 **CREATE IN ME A PURE HEART**

52. I trust in the lord – wicked boast

53. The fool says in his heart, "There is no God." Good looks down to see if any understand and seek God

54. Save Me by your name – Hear my prayer

55. distraught – thought to trouble me – the companion is evil – cast cares on the Lord, he will sustain you

56. Record my Lament – list my tears on your scroll

57. David flees from Saul to a cave – thank you for your protection

58. Even from birth, the wicked go astray – they are like snakes – Surely, there is a God who judges the earth. (When the wicked are punished)

59. Lord God Almighty, the God of Israel – words like swords from their mouth – you are my fortress

60. You have rejected us – give us aid

61. Increase the days of the king's life – I long to dwell in your tent forever

62. **MY SOUL FINDS REST IN GOD ALONE – MY SALVATION AND MY HONOR DEPEND ON GOD** – God is loving and strong

63. Oh God, you are my god, earnestly I seek you; **MY SOUL THIRSTS FOR YOU MORE**

64. Enemies are cunning – they encourage each other to do evil

65. **WHEN WE WERE OVERWHELMED WITH SIN, YOU FORGAVE** – you answer us with awesome deeds – praise God

66. SHOUT with joy to God, all the earth – Come see what God has done - **FOR YOU, O GOD, TESTED US;** refined us like silver, put us in prison – let me tell you what the lord has done for me

67. May god be gracious to us and bless us and make his face to shine upon us

68. God rides the skies – clouds – how awesome God has been to the faithful

69. **JESUS – THOSE WHO HATE ME WITHOUT REASON – ZEAL FOR YOUR HOUSE CONSUMES ME – THEY PUT GALL IN MY FOOD AND VINEGAR FOR MY THIRST**

70. short-come quickly to save me

71. Put enemies to shame

72. Last psalm prayer of David - **JESUS TO BLESS ALL NATIONS** - bless the king

Book III

73. **** **I ALMOST SLIPPED - I ENVIED THE ARROGANT -** pride is their necklace - you guide me - I was senseless and ignorant

74. Written after the temple was destroyed, asking God to come and destroy enemies - no prophets left, etc.,

75. wicked isare living it up -

76. make vows to the lord and fulfill them

77. consider gods past miracles - remember - **YOUR FOOTPRINTS WERE NOT SEEN** VS. 19

78. **Jesus** open my mouth with parables - vs. 25 men ate the bread of angels -- psalm recaps Egypt to David

79. Jerusalem **IN RUBBLE - NO ONE TO BURY THE DEAD**

80. restore us - **VS. 17 LET YOUR HAND REST ON THE MAN AT YOUR RIGHT HAND, THE SON OF MAN YOU HAVE RAISED UP FOR YOURSELF**

81. vs. 13 If my people would but listen - subdue enemies - fed with choice food

82. vs. 6 **YOU ARE GODS - SONS OF THE MOST HIGH**

83. deliver us from our enemies

84. **NO GOOD THING DOES HE WITHHOLD FROM THOSE WHOSE WALK IS BLAMELESS -** blessed is the man who trusts in you

85. **FAITHFULNESS FROM EARTH - RIGHTEOUSNESS FROM HEAVEN**

86. In the day of trouble, I will call for you, and you will answer me

87. the Lord loves Zion – people will say they were born in Zion

88. description of depression no friends and lots of darkness

89. Long psalm – **COVENANT WITH DAVID FOREVER** – but not for his sons –

Book IV

90. Psalm of Moses- A thousand years is like a day in your sight – men live to 70 – 80 if they have strength

91. acknowledge and love the lord, and he will rescue and protect us – vs. 14 because he loves me – I will rescue him

92. It is good to praise the Lord – wicked spring up like grass – evildoers flourish

93. the lord reigns

94. pay back the proud – **BLESSED IS THE MAN YOU DISCIPLINE** – anxiety was great, your consolation brought joy

95. the Israelites tested me in the desert, so they shall never enter my rest

96. Praise

97. Praise – love the lord, hate evil

98. Praise God with a new song – let the earth praise him

99. The lord reigns – **YOU WERE A FORGIVING GOD EVEN THOUGH YOU PUNISHED FOR MISDEEDS**

100. Know the Lord is God, and it is he who made us

101. I will have no part with evildoers

102. prayer of an afflicted man.

103. *****sins gone as far as east to west – satisfies all desires – forgives

104. Praise the Lord, O my soul - wine gladdens the heart, bread sustains his heart - when you send your spirit, they are created

105. remember the wonders of Abraham to the exodus

106. history of transgressions from exodus till now

Book V

107.   OVER AND OVER, GOD SAVES US FROM OUR OWN WICKEDNESS WHEN WE TURN TO HIM

108.   GIVE US AID AGAINST THE ENEMY, FOR THE HELP OF MAN IS WORTHLESS

109.   curse the evildoers – he wore cursing as a garment: it entered his body like water

110.   the Lord says to my Lord: "sit at my right hand until I make your enemies a footstool for your feet."

111.   follow his precepts fear is the beginning of wisdom

112.   blessed is the man that fears the lord and finds great delight in his commands

113.   God is Great

114.   tremble earth to the god of Jacob

115.   not to us but the glory to you – IDOLS CAN'T SPEAK, WALK, TOUCH, FEEL ETC THOSE WHO WORSHIP THEM WILL BE LIKE THEM

116.   I love the lord, for he heard my voice and helped me – How can I repay

117.   great is his love toward us

118.   *** Give thanks to the lord his love endures forever – set me free – chastened me severely but not given me over to death – THE STONE THE BUILDERS REJECTED HAS BECOME THE CAPSTONE – this is the day the lord has made - Give thanks

119.   Longest psalm –a- if only I could keep your precepts –b- THE WAY TO KEEP PURE –G-OPEN MY EYES THAT I MAY SEE WONDERFUL THINGS IN YOUR LAW – I am a stranger on earth –d- you have set my heart free –h- TURN MY EYES FROM WORTHLESS THINGS –w- I will answer the one who taunts me for I trust your word –z- this has been my practice I obey your precepts – h- I have considered my ways and have turned toward your statutes I am a friend to all who fear you –t- IT WAS GOOD

FOR ME TO BE AFFLICTED SO THAT I MIGHT LEARN YOUR DECREES –y- Your hands made me and formed me –k- when will you comfort me how long must I wait –l- IF NOT FOR YOUR LAW I WOULD HAVE PERISHED –m- your commands make me wiser I have more insight than my teachers –n- the wicked cause me harm but I will keep your statutes –s-I HATE DOUBLE MINDED MAN – a- deal with your servant according to your love –p- LET NO SIN RULE OVER ME –t- my zeal wears me out, YOUR PROMISES HAVE BEEN THOROUGHLY TESTED –o- I call out to you ; save me your statues established to last forever –r- look upon my suffering and deliver me – ss-I love your law –t- May my cry come before you, O lord - end

120. Too long have I lived among those who hate peace

121. the lord will watch over your life –

122. Jerusalem is a great city

123. we have endured much contempt. Have mercy

124. If the Lord had not been on our side

125. those who trust in the Lord are like mount Zion

126. Psalm of Joy for returning to Zion

127. UNLESS THE LORD HAS A HAND IN IT, IT IS DONE IN VAIN – CHILDREN ARE A REWARD

128. Blessed isare those who fear the lord – may you live to see your children's children

129. they have oppressed me but have not gained victory over me – plowmen have plowed my back

130. IF YOU KEEP A RECORD OF SINS, WHO CAN STAND – BUT WITH YOU THERE IS FORGIVENESS – MY SOUL WAITS FOR FORGIVENESS

131. My heart is not proud – I DO NOT CONCERN MYSELF WITH GREAT MATTERS

132. about the Lord's promises to David

133. How good it is when brothers live together in unity!!!

134. Blessing to ministers at night

135. I know the Lord is great – the idols are silver and gold – cannot see, hear, speak those who make them will be like them

136. His love endures forever – repeated many times – GIVES FOOD TO EVERY CREATURE

137. By the rivers of Babylon, we remember Zion – they ask for a song, but we hung our harps on the poplars

138. I will praise you with all my heart – you answered me and made me bold and stouthearted

139. **** You (God) are everywhere – I hate those that hate God – the misuse your name – TEST ME AND KNOW MY ANXIOUS THOUGHTS

140. do not let the wicked succeed in their plans, for they will become proud

141. SET A GUARD ON MY MOUTH, KEEP WATCH OVER MY LIPS – LET A RIGHTEOUS MAN STRIKE ME, IT IS A KINDNESS – let him rebuke me it is oil on my head

142. David in the cave – before him, I pour out my complaint, tell all my trouble

143. no one living is righteous before you – teach me to do your will – I remember the days of long ago

144. what is man that you care for him – I will sing a new song – deliver and rescue me

145. praise – the lord is gracious and compassionate, slow to anger, and rich in love – YOU SATISFY THE DESIRES OF EVERY LIVING THING

146. do not put trust in princess – sets prisoners free – a sight to the blind

147. THE LORD DELIGHTS IN THOSE WHO FEAR HIM WHO PUT THEIR HOPE IN HIS UNFAILING LOVE –

148. **** Praise him, sun and moon and shining stars

149. he crowns the humble with salvation

150. praise god with instruments and dancing – let everything that has breath praise the lord

Proverbs

1. purpose and theme – vs. **7 FEAR OF THE LORD IS THE BEGINNING OF KNOWLEDGE VS. 32 WAYWARDNESS WILL KILL, AND COMPLACENCY WILL DESTROY THEM**

2. moral benefits of wisdom – discretion will protect you vs. 11 – save you from the adulteress vs. 16 – she ignored the covenant she made

3. vs. 5 **TRUST IN THE LORD AND LEAN NOT ON YOUR UNDERSTANDING** vs. 8 this will bring health to your body vs. 9 honor the lord with your first fruits, make you overflow vs. 12 **THE LORD DISCIPLINES THOSE HE LOVES** vs. 25 have no fear of sudden disaster vs. 27 **DO NOT WITHHOLD GOOD FROM THOSE WHO DESERVE IT**

4. the right path is like the first gleam of dawn. The wrong path is darkness, and the wicked stumble over things they don't know vs. 18, 19 – **ABOVE ALL ELSE GUARD YOUR HEART** Vs. 23 - wisdom brings health to the whole body

5. warning against adultery – her paths are crooked, but she knows it not vs. 6 – **REJOICE IN THE WIFE OF YOUR YOUTH** a loving doe vs19

6. **HUMBLE YOURSELF IF YOU CAN'T MEET A PLEDGE – ANTS WORK HARD SO WORK HARD** – 6 things that are detestable to him including a man who stirs the brothers up – vs. 26 **PROSTITUTE REDUCES YOU TO A LOAF OF BREAD** – vs. 30, if a man steals from hunger, don't despise him

7. warning against adultery – she is loud and defiant – followed her like an ox to the slaughter – highway to the grave

8. I wisdom – wisdom precious – wisdom possess knowledge and discretion with prudence – those who seek me find me

9. Invitations of wisdom and folly – **WHOEVER CORRECTS A MOCKER OR A WICKED MAN INVITES ABUSE** – fear of the lord is the beginning of wisdom

10. start of proverbs **LAZY HANDS MAKE A POOR MAN** – wise accept commands chattering fool comes to ruin - conceal his hatred has lying lips – **WORDS ARE MANY, SIN IS NOT FAR BEHIND**

11. **PRIDE COMES THEN COMES DISGRACE – UNFAITHFUL TRAPPED BY EVIL DESIRES** – wicked men die all he expected from his power comes to nothing – a man lacks judgment derides his neighbor – **MANY ADVISORS MAKE VICTORY SURE** – put up security, and you will suffer – kindhearted woman gains respect – **GOLD RING IN PIGS SNOUT LIKE A BEAUTIFUL WOMAN WITHOUT DISCRETION – GENEROUS WILL PROSPER – TRUST IN RICHES AND YOU WILL FALL – <u>HE WHO WINS SOULS IS WISE</u> – RIGHTEOUS RECEIVE THEIR DUE ON EARTH**

12. a good man obtains favor from the Lord – **BETTER TO BE NOBODY AND HAVE A SERVANT THAN PRETEND TO BE SOMEBODY AND NOT HAVE FOOD** – he who chases fantasies lacks judgment – the way of a fool seems right to him – fool shows annoyance at once – prudent man keeps the knowledge to himself – **A DILIGENT MAN PRIZES HIS POSSESSIONS**

13. guard lips, guards his life – righteousness guards the man of integrity – **ONE PRETENDS TO BE RICH AND HAS NOTHING ANOTHER POOR AND IS RICH** – man's riches may pay his ransom, but a poor man hears no threat – **HE WHO GATHERS MONEY LITTLE BY LITTLE MAKES IT GROW** – fools detest turning from evil – companion of fools suffers harm – a good man leaves an inheritance – **SPARE THE ROD HATE HIS SON LOVE HIM CAREFUL TO DISCIPLINE**

14. the wise woman builds her house – mocker seeks wisdom and finds none – stay away from a foolish man – the wisdom of the prudent is to give thought to their ways – fools mock making amends for sin – **EACH HEART KNOWS ITS OWN BITTERNESS AND NO ONE ELSE CAN SHARE ITS JOY – <u>THERE IS A WAY THAT SEEMS RIGHT TO A MAN BUT IN THE END LEADS TO DEATH</u> – A SIMPLE MAN BELIEVES ANYTHING** – a fool is hotheaded and reckless –

rich have many friends – **ALL HARD WORK BRINGS PROFIT** – a patient man has great understanding – heart at peace gives great understanding – kindness to the needy honors God – even in death the righteous have a refuge

15. **GENTLE ANSWER TURNS AWAY WRATH** – eyes of the lord are everywhere – happy heart makes a cheerful face – the cheerful heart has a continual feast – **BETTER A LITTLE WITH FEAR OF THE LORD THAN GREAT WEALTH AND TURMOIL** – better a meal of veggies where there is love than a fattened calf with hatred - how good is a timely word – the lord tears down the proud man's house – **PURE THOUGHTS PLEASE THE LORD** – the righteous weighs its answers – good news gives health - **HUMILITY COMES BEFORE HONOR**

16. **MOTIVES ARE WEIGHED BY THE LORD – COMMIT TO THE LORD WHATEVER YOU DO** – Lord detests all the proud of heart – through love and faithfulness sin is atoned for – better a little with righteousness – **PRIDE GOES BEFORE DESTRUCTION** - better low in spirit and among the oppressed than to share plunder with the proud – there is a way that seems right to a man – the **LABORER'S APPETITE WORKS FOR HIM HIS HUNGER DRIVES HIM** - a gossip separates close friends – gray hair is a crown – **THE LOT IS CAST BUT IS EVERY DECISION IS FROM THE LORD**

17. Better a crust with peace and quiet than a house of feasting and strife,- **LORD TESTS THE HEART - COVER AN OFFENSE PROMOTES LOVE -** a friend loves at all times - do not put-up security - cheerful heart good medicine - use words with restraint even a fool appears wise when silent

18. **A FOOL DELIGHTS IN AIRING HIS OWN OPINIONS -** shame comes disgrace - one who is slack in his work is brother to one who destroys - **WEALTHY IMAGINE THEIR WALL UNSCALABLE** - gift opens the way - **CASTING LOTS SETTLES DISPUTES** - tongue has the power of life and death

19. **NOT GOOD TO HAVE ZEAL WITHOUT KNOWLEDGE -** man's folly ruins his life. Yet his heart rages against God - **QUARRELSOME WIFE IS LIKE CONSTANT DRIPPING** - a prudent wife is from the lord - **KIND TO POOR LENDS TO THE LORD** - a man desires unfailing love

20. **WINE BEER WHOEVER IS LEAD ASTRAY BY THEM IS NOT WISE - HONOR TO AVOID STRIFE** -- man's heart is deep waters a man of understanding draws them out - even a child is known by his actions - do not love sleep - **AVOID A MAN WHO TALKS TO MUCH** - do not say I will pay you back for this wrong - **TRAP TO DEDICATE SOMETHING RASHLY** - beatings purge the inmost being

21. **TO DO WHAT IS RIGHT IS MORE ACCEPTABLE THAN SACRIFICE** - plans lead to profit - better to live in the corner of a house - **LOVE PLEASURE BECOME POOR** - better to live in the desert - victory rest with the lord

22. see danger take refuge, simply keep going - drive out the mocker - **SLUGGARD SAY LION OUTSIDE I WILL BE MURDERED IN THE STREETS** - skilled man will serve kings - **DO NOT MAKE FRIENDS WITH HOT TEMPERED MAN**

23. If you falter in times of trouble, how small is your strength - **RESCUE THOSE BEING LED TO DEATH. DO NOT SAY I DIDN'T KNOW - RIGHTEOUS MAN FALLS 7 TIMES HE RISES AGAIN - DON'T GLOAT OVER OTHERS MISFORTUNE** - honest answer like a kiss on lips - don't pay back wrong deeds- slumber leads to scarcity

24. **DON'T EAT TOO MUCH - don't overstay your welcome - IF YOUR ENEMY IS HUNGRY, FEED HIM** - righteous not to give way to wicked - have self-control

25. Fools - lazy man - gossip - malicious man - **DON'T HIRE FOOLS** -fool wise in own eyes - **WITHOUT WOOD GOSSIP DIES OUT**

26. jealousy worse than anger and fury - **FULL YOU LOATHE HONEY** - blessings loud in the morning are taken as a curse - **MAN SHARPENS MAN** - man tested by praise - know the condition of your flocks

27. Rich man wise in own eyes - **CONCEAL SIN YOU WILL NOT PROSPER** - blessed is the man who always fears the lord - chasing fantasies leads to poverty - **HE WHO TRUST THE LORD WILL PROSPER**

28. the righteous care about justice for the poor- ruler listens to lies, his officials become wicked - a child left to himself disgraces his mother - a servant cannot be corrected with mere words - pamper a servant will bring grief - do not fear man trust the lord

29. do not add to gossips words - 2 **THINGS I ASK KEEP FALSEHOOD FROM ME MAKE ME NEITHER RICH nor POOR** - 4 things never satisfied grave barren womb land fire - 4 things I do not understand eagle snake ship move and a man with a maiden - 4 things earth cannot bear servant becomes king fool full of food unloved woman who is the married maid who displaces her mistress

30. Kings do not spend time on women and wine and beer - <u>**GIVE BEER TO THE POOR.**</u> - Wife of noble character

Ecclesiastes

1. Everything meaningless - wisdom meaningless

2. Pleasure, wisdom, folly toil meaningless - **VS. 24 A MAN DO NOTHING BETTER THAN EAT AND DRINK AND FIND SATISFACTION IN HIS WORK**

3. A time for everything - **GOD SET ETERNITY IN THE HEARTS OF MAN** - men are like animals. Both die. - Nothing better than to enjoy work

4. All labor and achievement come from envy of neighbor - 2 are better than one - 3 strands are not quickly broken

5. God is in heaven; you are on earth, let your words be few - who loves money never has enough - good for man to eat and drink and find satisfaction in his toil

6. **ENJOY YOUR PROSPERITY**

7. Wisdom - **DAY OF DEATH BETTER THAN BIRTH - WHO CAN STRAIGHTEN WHAT HE HAS MADE CROOKED BAD TIMES AND GOOD CONSIDER GOD HAS MADE THEM BOTH. - DO NOT BE OVER RIGHTEOUS** - everyone sins - don't pay attention to every word people say

8. **ENJOY LIFE** - even if a wise man claims he knows he really cannot comprehend it

9. Those who take oaths and those afraid to - enjoy life with your wife - one sinner destroys much - race not to swift battle to strong etc.

10. Lazy rafters sag - **MONEY ANSWER TO EVERYTHING** - don't curse king or rich a bird will carry it back

11. sow in the morning and work in the evening because you don't know which will succeed- **REMEMBER THE DAYS OF DARKNESS -**

12. **REMEMBER THE CREATOR IN YOUR YOUTH BEFORE TIMES OF TROUBLE** - desire no longer stirred - **SPIRIT RETURNS TO GOD WHO GAVE IT** - conclusion fear god and keep his commandments

Song of Songs

1. Do not stare at me because I am darkened by the sun - eyes are doves

2. Rose of Sharon lily of the valley - faint with love - **DO NOT AWAKEN LOVE UNTIL IT SO DESIRES**

3. I looked for my lover but could not find him-

4. Description of beloved - love better than wine -**YOU ARE A GARDEN LOCKED UP**

5. Open to me, my sister, my darling, my dove, my flawless one - went to look for lover and was beaten - description of the lover.

6. 60 queens and 80 concubines - virgins beyond number, but you are unique

7. Description of beloved - there I will give you my love

8. Left arm under head right embraces me - **LOVE IS AS STRONG AS DEATH - MY OWN VINEYARD IS MINE TO GIVE -**

Isaiah

1. A rebellious nation - **STOP BRINGING MEANINGLESS OFFERINGS - SINS ARE LIKE SCARLET; THEY SHALL BE WHITE AS SNOW -** rebel and sinner both be broken

2. He will judge between nations - idols they bow down to the work of their hands -pride will be humbled - **STOP TRUSTING IN MAN**

3. You have a cloak; you be our leader no - women of Zion haughty

4. 7 women will want 1 man's name

5. The vineyard - 6 woes, including **CHAMPIONS OF MIXED DRINKS**

6. Isaiah sees the lord like in revelations - **HERE AM I SEND ME,**

7. **IF YOU DO NOT STAND FIRM IN YOUR FAITH, YOU WILL NOT STAND AT ALL - VIRGIN BIRTH** of Immanuel

8. Married Prophetess and gave birth to Maher-Shalal-Hash-Baz – **FEAR GOD, NOT MEN** – consult God, not mediums, spiritualists, or the dead

9. **GALILEE TO BE HONORED – TO US A CHILD IS BORN – WONDERFUL COUNSELOR MIGHTY GOD -** god's anger against Israel

10. Woe to Assyria's king. He is full of pride – does the ax raise itself above him who swings it? - Zion, do not be afraid of the Assyrians. The Lord will strike the warriors with a sickness

11. The branch of Jesse – the branch will have the spirit wisdom, poser and counsel and the fear of the Lord – **THE LORD WILL REACH OUT A SECOND TIME AND RECLAIM THE REMNANT**

12. Surely, the Lord is my salvation. I will not be afraid – Let this be known to the entire world

13. The Lord is mustering an army against Babylon – Terror will seize them – every man's heart will melt – Babylon will be overthrown by God like Sodom and Gomorrah

14. Once again, God will choose Israel - **ALIENS WILL JOIN THEM** -- prophecy against Babylon, Assyria, and the Philistines

15. Prophecy against Moab

16. Moab continued - vs. 5 in love a throne will be established - vs. 14 in 3 years Moab will be gone

17. Damascus to be destroyed - Jacob will fade - in that day men will look to their maker leave their false gods - uproar of the peoples like great waters

18. Prophecy against Cush -

19. Prophecy ABOUT Egypt - rivers dry up - alters to the Lord in the heart of Egypt - **vs. 25 BLESSED BE EGYPT MY PEOPLE, ASSYRIA MY HANDIWORK, AND ISRAEL MY INHERITANCE.**

20. Prophecy against Egypt and Cush - people who trusted in these countries will be disappointed and afraid- **ISAIAH NAKED FOR 3 YEARS AS A SIGN**

21. P against Babylon - fallen - p against Edom and Arabia

22. P about Jerusalem - made preparations against attack but gave no regard to the lord - said let us eat and drink tomorrow we die -- **THIS SIN WILL NOT BE ATONED FOR** - make him a peg then shear it off

23. P against Tyre – almighty planned it to bring the low the pride of all glory – to humble all who are renowned

24. **DEVASTATION OF THE ENTIRE EARTH** – will punish the powers in the heavens above and the kings on the earth below

25. Praise to the Lord – swallow up death – **SURELY THIS IS OUR GOD WE TRUSTED IN HIM, AND HE SAVED US** – Moab trampled like straw is trampled down in the manure

26. the nation that keeps faith you will keep in perfect peace him whose mind is steadfast because he trusts you – fire reserved for your enemies consume them = **YOUR DEAD WILL LIVE THEIR BODIES WILL RISE**

27. A calling of Israel – deliverance

28. Woe to Ephraim – stagger from wine and beer – the understanding of this message will bring sheer terror

29. Woe to Jerusalem – **PREDICTION OF JESUS** – people honor me with their lips, but their hearts are far from me – worship is made up

of rules taught by men – **POT SAYS TO POTTER HE KNOWS NOTHING** – blind will see – wayward in spirit will gain understanding

30. woe to the obstinate nation and children - woe to you for forming an alliance with Egypt instead of the Lord – **THEY SAY NO MORE VISIONS OR PROPHECY. TELL US PLEASANT THINGS – STOP CONFRONTING US WITH THE HOLY ONE** – in repentance and rest is your salvation, quietness, and trust is your strength – **THE LORD LONGS TO BE GRACIOUS TO YOU** – blessed are all who wait for him – **THROW YOUR IDOLS LIKE A MENSTRUAL CLOTH** – the lord will cause men to hear his voice

31. Woe to those who rely on Egypt – he who helps will stumble – he who is helped will stumble – Assyria will fall by a sword that is not of man – a sword not of man will devour them – commanders will panic

32. the kingdom of righteousness – eyes of those who see will no longer be closed – stammering tongue will be fluent – women who are complacent, trouble is coming – till the spirit is poured on us – **FRUIT OF RIGHTEOUS WILL BE PEACE, QUIETNESS, AND CONFIDENCE FOREVER**

33. Distress and help – when you stop destroying, you will be destroyed – the Lord is our judge, our king, our lawgiver; he will save us – sins of those who dwell in Jerusalem will be forgiven

34. Judgment against the nations – Edom will become a desert

35. Joy – highway will be there – it will be called the Way of Holiness – they will enter Zion with singing

36 - 37 Sennacherib of Assyria goes against Jerusalem – **THE ASSYRIAN KING ASKS WHO DO YOU TRUST IN – DON'T TRUST GOD -** the remnant is saved, and 185,000 men of Assyria killed the king killed by his sons

38. Hezekiah's illness – and **WRITING AFTER HIS ILLNESS AND RECOVERY BY HEZEKIAH**

39. Hezekiah shows everything to the envoys from Babylon

40. **JOHN THE BAPTIST PREDICTED** - who can you compare the lord to

41. Israel is my servant - try and get an idol to do anything it can't; they are less than nothing

42. **A LIGHT TO THE GENTILES** - new things I declare - who is blind but my servant - you have seen many things but paid no attention

43. Before me no God was formed, and none will follow – Forget the former things do not dwell on the past – **YET YOU HAVE NOT CALLED ON ME YOU HAVE NOT WEARIED YOURSELVES FOR ME, BUT YOU HAVE BURDENED ME WITH YOUR SINS AND WEARIED ME WITH YOUR OFFENSES** – I BLOT OUT YOUR TRANSGRESSIONS FOR MY OWN SAKE AND REMEMBER YOUR SINS NO MORE

44. Israel and Jerusalem to be rebuilt – I pour out my spirit on your offspring – **A GREAT DESCRIPTION OF A MAN AND HIS IDOL – A DELUDED HEART MISLEADS HIM; HE CANNOT SAVE HIMSELF**

45. **DOES THE CLAY SAY TO THE POTTER WHAT ARE YOU MAKING?** - Turn to me and be saved all you end of the earth

46. Gods of Babylon – from that spot it cannot move – it cannot save him from his troubles – I say my purpose will stand from a far-off land a man to fulfill my purpose

47. fall of Babylon – comes quickly – **YOUR WISDOM AND KNOWLEDGE WILL MISLEAD YOU** – Astrologers come forward and cannot save you

48. **VS. 10 I HAVE REFINED YOU, THOUGH NOT AS SILVER; I HAVE TESTED YOU IN THE FURNACE OF AFFLICTION** – I am the Lord … who teaches you what is best for you who directs you in the way you should go – IF YOU PAID ATTENTION TO MY COMMANDS YOUR PEACE WOULD BE LIKE A RIVER

49. **IT IS TOO SMALL A THING FOR YOU, MY SERVANT, TO RESTORE THE TRIBES OF JACOB AND BRING BACK THOSE OF ISRAEL I HAVE KEPT. I WILL ALSO MAKE YOU A LIGHT FOR THE GENTILES, THAT YOU MAY BRING SALVATION TO THE ENDS OF THE EARTH VS. 6**

50. Where is your mother's certificate of divorce – because of your sins, you were sold – Was my arm too short to ransom you – Do I lack the

strength to rescue you? I offered my back to those who beat me – I know I will not be put to shame.

51. Salvation for all time - **DO NOT BE SCARED OF MORTAL MEN**

52. All the ends of the earth will see the salvation of our God – the servant will be raised and lifted up and highly exalted – vs. 15 FOR **WHAT THEY WERE NOT TOLD THEY WILL SEE, AND WHAT THEY HAVE NOT HEARD, THEY WILL UNDERSTAND**

53. <u>**CHRIST ON THE CROSS!!!!!**</u>

54. A wife married young only to be rejected - this is like the day of Noah now I have sworn not to be angry with you again - I have created the destroyer to work havoc

55. Thirsty free wine - **SEEK THE LORD WHILE HE MAY BE FOUND-** a word that goes out will not return to me empty

56. **FOREIGNERS TO BE SAVED** - I will gather still others to them besides those already gathered - **WICKED LOVE SLEEP AND BEER**

57. **righteous taken to be spared from evil** - made your bed and went there to offer sacrifices made a pact with those whose beds you love - you were wearied by all your ways but would not say it is hopeless - <u>**I LIVE IN A HOLY PLACE BUT ALSO WITH HIM WHO IS CONTRITE AND LOWLY IN SPIRIT -**</u> there is no peace for the wicked

58. **TRUE FASTING** - share your food with the hungry - shelter - clothe - then your healing will quickly appear - the Sabbath is a delight; do it right

59. Bad spin a spider's web of lies - the lies web is useless as clothing - we confess we are bad - **GOD INTERVENED - PUT ON BREASTPLATE HELMET GARMENTS CLOAK**

60. Glory of Zion

61. the spirit is on me to preach the good news to the poor, release from darkness the captives – bestow on them beauty, gladness, garment of praise – you will be called priest of God and named ministers of our god – clothed me with garments of salvation, the robe of

righteousness, adorned my head like a bridegroom like a bride adorns herself with jewels

62. Zion's new name

63. Red garments of God because of the blood of nations - no one helped God - they rebelled and grieved the Holy Spirit - he who set the Holy Spirit among them - given rest by the Holy Spirit - you harden our hearts

64. **YOU DID AWESOME THINGS THAT WE DID NOT EXPECT -** you help those who gladly do right - **WE ARE CLAY YOU ARE POTTER -** don't remember our sins -temple burned in the fire

65. Obstinate people will receive gods' full payment for their deeds - a remnant will not be destroyed - servants will eat, you will go hungry - I will create new heavens, new earth - **THEY CALL I WILL ANSWER WHILE THEY ARE STILL SPEAKING**

66. **I ESTEEM HE WHO IS HUMBLE AND CONTRITE IN SPIRIT AND TREMBLES AT MY WORD -** can a country be born in a day or a nation in a moment - flourish like grass - all-mankind will come and bow

Jeremiah

1. During Josiah to Zedekiah to the exile - God touched his mouth and put his words there - don't be afraid; I am with you

2. go to Jerusalem - what fault did your fathers find in me - priest did not ask where the lord is - has a nation ever changed its god -2 sins forsaken me and dug their own cisterns - brought this on yourselves by forsaken me - **IN VAIN I PUNISHED YOUR PEOPLE THEY DID NOT RESPOND TO CORRECTION- <u>HOW SKILLED YOU ARE AT PURSUING LOVE</u> EVEN THE WORST WOMEN CAN LEARN FROM YOUR WAYS**

3. you have lived as a prostitute with many lovers - **IS THERE ANY PLACE WHERE YOU HAVE NOT BEEN RAVISHED - PRAY WELL BUT DO ALL THE EVIL YOU CAN -** gave Israel a divorce - Judah's unfaithful sister did not return to me with all her heart but only in pretense - **<u>THE ARK WILL NOT BE MISSED, OR ANOTHER ONE MADE</u>**

4. Circumcise your hearts - lord completely deceived these people, saying you have peace - your own conduct and actions brought this upon you - my people are fools skilled in doing evil - no people land destroyed towns deserted

5. **IF YOU FIND ONE PERSON WHO DEALS HONESTLY AND SEEKS THE TRUTH, I WILL SPARE THE CITY - REFUSE TO REPENT -** sworn by gods that are not gods - thronged the houses of prostitutes - **LIED ABOUT THE LORD SAYING HE WILL DO NOTHING -** distant ancient nation against you - as you have forsaken me and served other gods ....- Eyes but do not see ears but do not hear

6. Jerusalem full of wickedness - **WORD OF THE LORD IS OFFENSIVE TO THEM - <u>LEAST TO GREATEST GREEDY FOR GAIN</u> -** no shame in their conduct - **ASK WHERE THE GOOD WAY IS AND WALK IN IT AND YOU WILL FIND REST FOR YOUR SOULS -** I will put obstacles before this people - I have made you a tester of metals

7. Reform - do not trust in deceptive words and say this is the temple of the lord this is .... **- MY HOUSE HAS BECOME A DEN OF**

ROBBERS - do not worship the queen of heaven - I did not only give them instructions on burnt offerings hut to obey me - **DAY AFTER DAY I SENT YOU PROPHETS, BUT YOU DID NOT LISTEN** - valley of slaughter

8. Bones of everyone exposed - they cling to deceit. I have listened attentively, but they don't say what is right; no one repents - since they rejected the word, what kind of wisdom do they have - least to .... **GREEDY FOR GAIN** - my comforter in sorrow my heart is faint within me - is there no balm in Gilead

9. my head were a spring, my eyes fountains so l could weep day and night - they go from one sin to another - **WEARY THEMSELVES WITH SINNING** - I will refine and test them what else can l do - boast about this he understands and knows me ...

10. do not be terrified by signs in the sky - customs of the people are worthless - **DO NOT FEAR IDOLS THEY CAN DO NO HARM - INQUIRE OF THE LORD AND PROSPER** - Jer. prayer - man's life not his own **CORRECT ME BUT ONLY WITH JUSTICE NOT IN YOUR ANGER**

11. Covenant is broken - you have many gods - as many as towns in Judah and streets in Jerusalem - **DO NOT PRAY** or offer a plea or petition.... - Plot against Jeremiah - led like a lamb to slaughter - **WANTED HIM TO STOP PREACHING**

12. Why do the wicked prosper? – You are always on their lips but far from their hearts. Yet you know me, O Lord, you see me **AND TEST MY THOUGHTS ABOUT YOU.** - If you raced men on foot and tired, how can you compete with horses? – do not trust them though they speak well of you. – As for the wicked, I will uproot them

13. **LINEN BELT – BURIED AND DUG UP** becomes useless, so has Judah become completely useless – wineskins – wineskins should be full – **GOD TO MAKE EVERYONE DRUNK AND HATE EACH OTHER** – captivity to come – do not be arrogant – if you do not listen because of your pride I will weep secretly and bitterly – Why has this happened to ME **BECAUSE OF YOUR MANY SINS CAN A LEOPARD CHANGE ITS SPOTS NEITHER CAN YOU DO GOOD WHO ARE ACCUSTOMED TO DOING EVIL** – your adulteries and lustful neighing's your shameless

prostitution I have seen your detestable acts on the hills and in the fields

14. **<u>DO NOT PRAY FOR THE WELL-BEING OF THIS PEOPLE.</u>** Although they fast and offer burnt offerings, I will not listen – Prophets arc telling lics that all will be peace – **THEY ARE DELUSIONAL** they will die by the sword or famine – **DO THE SKIES THEMSELVES SEND RAIN NO IT IS YOU O LORD OUR GOD**

15. Even if Moses and Samuel were to stand in before me, my heart would not go out to this people – because of what Manasseh son of Hezekiah, king of Judah did – When your words came, I ate them they were my Joy and my heart's delight – **IF YOU REPENT, I WILL RESTORE YOU** and make you my spokesman and protect you from them

16. Do not marry because disaster is coming - why because of sins - time will come surely as the lord lives who brought us out of Egypt but.... who brought us out of the north

17. **CURSED IS THE ONE WHO TRUSTS IN MAN - BLESSED IS THE MAN WHO TRUSTS IN THE LORD** - the lord searches the heart and examines the mind to reward according to his conduct to what his deeds deserve - heal me, and I will be healed save me ...- keep the Sabbath holy

18. Potter house - observe as the potter makes a pot, and it is marred, he shapes it into another pot - **REPENT AND I WILL RELENT** - people plan to attack Jeremiah

19. Buy a clay pot, then break the jar and say the lord will smash this nation, and <u>IT WILL NOT BE REPAIRED</u>

20. <u>PASHHUR HAS JEREMIAH BEATEN -</u> **JEREMIAH SPEAKS OF HIS PROBLEMS AND PRAISES GOD**

21. **KING ZEDEKIAH ASKS JEREMIAH TO SEE IF THE LORD WILL PERFORM WONDERS ... AS IN TIMES PAST....-** whoever stays in the city will die; whoever leaves will be taken in captivity

22. Woe to kings - Shallum - Jehoiakim - Jehoiachin -

23. **I WILL BRING THEM BACK WITH A SPECIAL SHEPARD** - evil and lying and adulterous priests and prophets - they tell lies

and tell each other their dreams - FALSE **PROPHETS EVERY MAN'S OWN WORD BECOMES HIS ORACLE AND SO YOU DISTORT THE WORDS OF GOD**

24. 2 baskets of figs - good figs represent the god Jews to be watched over by God

25. **THOUGH THE LORD HAS SENT ALL HIS SERVANTS, THE PROPHETS, TO YOU AGAIN AND AGAIN, YOU HAVE NOT LISTENED**.... Babylon to conquer all the nations of the earth to last 70 years -

26. Jeremiah prophesies in the temple **SEIZED BY PRIEST AND PEOPLE TO BE PUT TO DEATH -** spared - King Jehoiakim killed Uriah for saying the same things earlier

27. All nations, including Judah, to serve Nebuchadnezzar and Babylon – **DON'T LISTEN TO LYING PROPHETS WHO SAY DON'T WORRY ABOUT BABYLON – DON'T FRET OVER THE ARTICLES TAKEN FROM THE TEMPLE BE CONCERNED THAT THE REST OF THE ARTICLES WON'T BE TAKEN**

28. False Prophet – <u>HANANIAH BREAKS THE YOKE AROUND JEREMIAH'S NECK AND TELLS EVERYONE THAT THEY WILL BE FREE OF BABYLON IN TWO YEARS – JEREMIAH TELLS HIM THAT HE WILL DIE THIS YEAR – HE DIES IN THE 7TH MONTH</u>

29. letter to exiles - you will be there 70 years, so increase in number - the ones left behind will die - **PRAY FOR THE PLACE TO PROSPER SO THAT YOU WILL PROSPER** - more false prophets- one wants Jeremiah locked up

30. Restoration of Israel - the wound is incurable, no healing for you - but I will restore your health - in days to come, you will understand

31. I will build up again – they will pray as I bring them back – the Lord will create a new thing on earth, a woman will surround a man – vs. 30 **INSTEAD EVERYONE WILL DIE FOR HIS OWN SIN – NEW COVENANT – I WILL PUT MY LAW IN THEIR MINDS AND ON THERE HEARTS NO LONGER WILL A MAN TEACH HIS BROTHER OR NEIGHBOR BECAUSE THEY WILL ALL KNOW ME** – Jerusalem will never again be uprooted or demolished

32. King Zedekiah asks Jeremiah why he always prophecies against him – Jeremiah tells him that God told him to buy a field and that he will bring prosperity back

33. vs. 3 **CALL TO ME AND I WILL ANSWER YOU AND TELL YOU GREAT AND UNSEARCHABLE THINGS YOU DO NOT KNOW** – the city will be desolate, but in the future, it will prosper - vs. 9 then this city will bring me renown, joy, praise, and honor before all nations on earth – **DAVID'S BRANCH WILL PRODUCE THE ONE CALLED THE LORD OUR RIGHTEOUSNESS** – David will always have a descendant on the throne

34. Zedekiah warned about Babylon – Freedom to Hebrew slaves – then the Jews recaptured them – God then gave them 'Freedom' to die by the sword

35. <u>**THE RACABITES** OBEYED THEIR FATHERS AND DID NOT DRINK WINE</u> or plant but lived in tents – God held them up as an example of what Israel should obey God's Laws – God then blessed the tribe

36. **JEHOIAKIM, KING OF JUDAH, BURNS THE SCROLL JEREMIAH DICTATED TO BARUCH** – Jeremiah and Baruch hide because the king wants them arrested – they rewrite the scroll – the king showed no fear or remorse as he cut the scroll and burnt it

37. Zedikiah had been made king by Nebuchadnezzar – neither he nor the priest nor the people would listen to Jeremiah – **JEREMIAH FALSELY ACCUSED OF DESERTION AND SENT TO PRISON** – King calls him after a long time and asks if any word from God – Jeremiah tells him Yea you are going to be handed over to Babylon

38. **JEREMIAH LOWERED INTO A CISTERN SANK IN MUD LEFT TO STARVE** – king said he would not oppose them – a Cushite comes to the king and pleads to let him go – the king says ok and take 30 men to get him out – the king secretly goes to Jeremiah and asks what the lord says – he tells him to surrender and live refuse and everything will be destroyed – king tells Jeremiah to tell officials that he wanted to be sent back to someone's house instead of the truth – **THE KING WAS AFRAID OF THE JEWS ALREADY IN CAPTIVITY IN BABYLON**

39. Fall of Jerusalem - **KING ZEDEKIAH CAPTURED EYES PUT OUT AFTER HE SEES HIS SONS PUT TO DEATH** - Ebed-Melech the Cushite spared because he trusts in the Lord

40. **JEREMIAH CAPTURED AND FREED** by the Babylonians - Governor Gedaliah assassinated

41-42. Ishmael is hunted down by the guards - he flees, but everyone he captured goes back to the guards - they are scared and ask Jeremiah what God wants them to do - 10 days later, God tells them to go back to Jerusalem

43. **THEY CALL HIM A LIAR AND GO TO EGYPT** - God tells Jeremiah to bury 2 stones in front of the pharaoh's palace - that is where Neb. is going to set his tent when he takes Egypt

44. Warning that they will die - they refuse to listen and say they will continue to serve the queen of heaven - sign will be the fall of the pharaoh

45. Message for Baruch - let escape

46. message about Egypt - I will destroy pharaoh Egypt her gods, and those who rely on Pharaoh

47. Message about Philistines - calls Philistines remnant also

48. Message about Moab - since you trust your deeds and riches, you too will be taken captive - yet l will restore your fortunes

49. message about ammonites - destroy and restore - message about Edom - strip Esau bare - I swear by myself - message about Damascus - message about Kedar and Hazor

50. 50-51. message about Babylon - people of Israel and Judah will go in tears to seek the Lord - do to her Babylon as she has done to others - I will forgive the remnant I spare - I set a trap for Babylon -- **VENGEANCE FOR THE TEMPLE** - idols that will go mad with terror - I will stir up the spirit of a destroyer - **RUN FOR YOUR LIVES** - every man is senseless and without knowledge, every goldsmith is ashamed by his idol - no rock to be made a cornerstone - do not lose heart when you hear rumors - leave and do not linger - **BECAUSE FOREIGNERS ENTERED THE HOLY PLACES** - Jeremiah told the official to read in Babylon and then throw in the river

51. History of the fall of Jerusalem - **JEREMIAH WAS KING ZEDEKIAH'S FATHER-IN-LAW**

Lamentations

1. The enemy laid hands on all her treasures. **SHE SAW PAGAN NATIONS ENTER HER SANCTUARY**

2. cloud of his anger – he has not remembered his footstool – fierce anger spurned both king and priest – the **LORD REJECTED HIS ALTER AND ABANDONED HIS SANCTUARY** – the visions OF **YOUR PROPHETS WERE FALSE AND WORTHLESS THEY DID NOT EXPOSE YOUR SIN TO WARD OFF YOUR CAPTIVITY** – the city that was called the perfection of beauty – should women eat their offspring should priest and prophet be killed in the sanctuary of the Lord?

3. Even when I cry out for help, he shuts out my prayer – mangled me- I have been deprived of peace. I have forgotten what prosperity is – **THEY ARE NEW EVERY MORNING GREAT IS YOUR FAITHFULNESS – THE LORD IS GOOD TO THOSE WHOSE HOPE IS IN HIM – LET HIM OFFER HIS CHEEK TO ONE WHO WOULD STRIKE HIM** – from the Most High that both calamities and good come from – **WHY SHOULD ANY MAN COMPLAIN WHEN PUNISHED FOR HIS SINS – LET US EXAMINE OUR WAYS AND TEST THEM** – they tried to end my life in a pit

4. once worth their weight in gold – punishment of my people is greater than that of Sodom – skin white and pink now black and dried up – it has become like a stick – **COMPASSIONATE WOMEN HAVE COOKED THEIR OWN CHILDREN** – kindled a fire that consumed Zion – but it happened because of the sins of her prophets and the iniquities of her priests

5. We must buy water to drink – Our fathers sinned, and we bear their punishment – Our skin is hot as an oven…. Women and virgins have been ravished – Restore us to yourself…. unless you have utterly rejected us and are angry with us beyond measure

Ezekiel

1. **5TH YEAR OF EXILE** - saw a vision - saw 4 winged creatures - followed by wheels - saw God in his glory

2. The Lord tells Ezekiel he must speak to the rebellious nation

3. Ate the scroll with the words from God tasted like honey – Israel not willing to listen, but I will make you harder than them – overwhelmed sat for 7 days – **WARN THE WICKED OR YOU WILL BE HELD ACCOUNTABLE** – shut yourself in your house

4. **DREW JERUSALEM ON A CLAY TABLET AND LAY NEXT TO IT FOR 390 DAYS FOR ISRAEL AND 40 DAYS FOR JUDAH'S YEARS OF SIN – ATE FOOD COOKED OVER COW EXCREMENT**

5. I am so mad at this nation – **YOU HAVE NOT EVEN CONFORMED TO THE STANDARDS OF THE NATIONS AROUND YOU** – I will do to you what I have never done before and will never do again

6. I will destroy the high places (idol worship) – I will slay people in front of your idols … - but I will spare some – he that is far away will die of the plague; he that is near will fall by the sword and he that survives will die by famine

7. **THE END IS HERE!** – The Lord says: The end! – The Lord says: **DISASTER! – THE END HAS COME! – THEIR SILVER AND GOLD WILL NOT BE ABLE TO SAVE THEM… FOR IT HAS MADE THEM STUMBLE**

8. **GOD TAKES EZEKIEL TO MANY PLACES TO SEE THE DETESTABLE ACTS** – Saw an Idol of jealousy – saw the elders each at the shrine of his own idol in the darkness – woman morning Tammuz (idol) – 25 men worshiping the sun

9. God commands 6 MEN **TO KILL EVERYONE THAT DOES NOT HAVE A MARK ON HIS FOREHEAD** – A man in linen was to mark the good people

10. **THE GLORY OF THE LORD DEPARTS THE TEMPLE**

11. 25 men said is it not time to build houses – the city is a cooking pot, and we are the meat – You have killed many – they are the meat, but I will drive you out – while prophesying Pelatiah died – apparently, he was related I think he was good – Israel promised to be brought back – **I WILL GIVE THEM AN UNDIVIDED HEART AND A NEW SPIRIT IN THEM**

12. Exile symbolized by **EZEKIEL GOING THROUGH THE WALL** – He says the prince will go the same way – **MANY PEOPLE START SAYING WHAT HE SAYS IS FOR THE DISTANT FUTURE** – the Lord says they will all be fulfilled now

13. False prophets condemned – women use magic charms and veils to ensnare men

14. Idolaters condemned – if an idolater inquires of the Lord, he will only hear Repent! – Judgment inescapable – **IF NOAH, DANIEL, AND JOB** were all here, they would be the only ones to escape their children, and wives would not – some will survive, and you will be consoled by their conduct and actions

15. **JERUSALEM A USELESS VINE** – branches of trees are better – **AFTER IT HAS BEEN BURNED IT IS EVEN MORE USELESS**

16. Unfaithful Jerusalem like a prostitute or adulterous wife – **VERY TOUCHING DESCRIPTION OF HOW HE BROUGHT JERUSALEM UP TO BECOME THE MOST BEAUTIFUL QUEEN** – were even lewder than Sodom – **SODOM SINS INCLUDE ARROGANCE, OVERFED, UNCONCERNED, DID NOT HELP THE POOR, HAUGHTY AND DID DETESTABLE THINGS** – I will make for you and all that you have done

17. Two eagles – the tip of tree transplanted one to a fertile field – easy to pull up – another to the top of a mountain – every tree will know that the lowly tree will become high and the big tree will wither away – first vine or twig went to Babylon

18. The soul who sins will die - **DESCRIPTION OF RIGHTEOUS MAN** - good man turns to evil, then he will die - **BAD REPENTS WILL LIVE** - you say the way of the Lord is not just - **REPENT AND LIVE**

19. Lament for Israel

20. **SINS STARTED IN EGYPT** - brought idols with them - utterly desecrated my Sabbaths - their hearts devoted to idols - blasphemed me by forsaking me - bring you back purge you of those who rebel against me - I deal with you for the sake of my own name - flame to devour everything - **JUST TELLING PARABLES**

21. Babylon to be God's sword - testing will come - king of Babylon will use lots to determine who to attack next - punishment reached its climax

22. **JERUSALEM'S SINS** - shed blood makes idols desecrated, the Sabbaths eat at shrines, commit lewd acts, dishonor father's bed, etc.

23. 2 adulterous sisters - Samaria and Jerusalem - worse than Sodom - **GENITALS LIKE DONKEYS**

24. Cooking pot - can't cook out Jerusalem's impurity - **IMPURITY IS LEWDNESS - EZEKIEL'S WIFE DIES**

25. Prophecy against Ammon Moab Edom Philistia

26. Prophecy against Tyre - end to noisy songs - to be thrown in a pit - make you dwell in the earth below

27. Lament for Tyre

28. **PROPHECY AGAINST KING OF TYRE - SAYS HE IS A GOD** - description of king and Satan - prophecy against Sidon

29. Prophecy against Egypt – **DESTROYED COMPLETELY FOR 40 YEARS, THEN RESTORED BUT NEVER AS A MAJOR NATION AGAIN** – Nebuchadnezzar to destroy Egypt as a reward for trying to destroy Tyre

30. Lament for Egypt – the allies of Egypt will fall – I will destroy the idols

31. Cedar in Lebanon – Pharaoh is the Cedar – the tallest tree is him – destined for death to go down to the pit

32. Lament for Pharaoh – I snuff you out – they go down to the pit of the uncircumcised – Assyria, Elam, Meshech and Tubal, Pharaoh, Edom, Princes of the north and the Sidonians there – although I had him spread terror in the land of the living Pharaoh will be there

33. Ezekiel a watchman – wicked repent they will be saved when righteous sin they will die. – if the watchman doesn't warn and they die, he is held accountable if he does warn, he is not accountable –

each according to his own ways – Jerusalem's fall explained – a man escaped to tell that the city had fallen – Ezekiel able to talk again – **ABRAHAM ONLY ONE MAN BUT POSSESSED THE LAND WE ARE MANY HOW COME WE CAN'T – REASON MANY SINS** – country men telling people to Listen to Ezekiel – **EXPRESS DEVOTION BUT HEARTS ARE GREEDY, TO THEM YOU ARE NOTHING MORE THAN ONE WHO SINGS LOVE SONGS AND PLAYS AN INSTRUMENT WELL, THEY HEAR BUT DO NOT PUT THE WORDS TO PRACTICE**

34. Woe to the shepherd of Israel who only takes care of themselves! You have not strengthened the weak or healed the sick – **I AM AGAINST THE SHEPHERDS AND WILL HOLD THEM ACCOUNTABLE** – I will bind up the weak sheep and destroy the sleek and strong – I will judge between the fat and the lean sheep – **I WILL PLACE OVER THEM ONE SHEPHERD MY SERVANT DAVID, AND HE WILL TEND THEM** – bring showers of blessings – the sheep are people, and I am your God

35. Prophecy against Edom – I will treat you in accordance with the anger and jealousy you showed in your hatred of them

36. Prophecy to the mountains of Israel – I swear with uplifted hand that the nations around you will also suffer scorn – defiled the land with their conduct and their actions – I restore Israel not for your sake but for the sake of my holy name – I will sprinkle clean water on you, and you will be clean – **I WILL GIVE YOU A NEW HEART AND A NEW SPIRIT -** They will say "this land that was laid waste has become like the garden of Eden

37. Valley of the bones – God brings Israel back to life! One nation under one king – Ezekiel takes one stick and writes on it Judah another stick and writes on it Ephraim – told to combine sticks to become one – **WILL MAKE JUDAH AND EPHRAIM ONE NATION AGAIN ISRAEL – ONE KING OVER THEM NEVER DIVIDED AGAIN** – make Israel holy again

38. Prophecy against Gog – they see an unprotected country, Israel, and decide to attack – When Gog attacks Israel, my hot anger will be aroused – **I WILL CAUSE AN EARTHQUAKE** – I will summon a sword against Gog

39. Gog will be defeated – Israel to use their weapons as full for 7 years – **7 MONTHS TO BURY THEM** – animals will gorge themselves

on the dead – I will no longer hide my face from Israel I will pour out my spirit on them

40 – 42. New Temple area detailed description – priests Levites sons of Zadok – A most holy place – temple decorated with cherubs, palm trees, and lions

43. Glory returns to the temple – I will live among them forever – instructions on the alter and how to dedicate it

44. the prince may enter one door that no others enter – because some Levites brought uncircumcised in heart and flesh into my sanctuary and practiced worship to idols, they may not come near but work in the outside areas – only Levites descended of Zadok may come near – priests are now judges – they are not to own anything but live on what is given to God.

45. Division of the land – my princes will no longer oppress the people. Offerings and holy days

46. Prince to enter on one door only to him – open only on the Sabbaths and new moons – Prince gifts to his son are passed on to next generation – gifts to servants are returned when they are freed – Prince not to take any inheritance of the people

47. The river from the temple – the river will go to the sea – the fruit will grow but not fall, and the leaves will be used to heal – Boundaries of the land

48. Division of the land – the city will have 3 gates on each of 4 sides – each will bear the name of a tribe of Israel – the name of the city will be, THE LORD IS THERE

Daniel

1. Daniel and others in Nebuchadnezzar's custody – 4 men, Daniel and Shadrach, Meshach, and Abednego eat only vegetables – God gives them great understanding – the king says they are 10 times smarter than anyone

2. Nebuchadnezzar's dream – all wise men ordered to tell the king his dream then interpret it – got impatient and ordered all wise men killed – Daniel was to be killed went to the king asked for time to interpret – prayed to God and the mystery was revealed – told the king and he was amazed – the dream was the huge statue of gold (head) silver bronze iron then feet of clay and iron – a stone breaks the statue and becomes a mountain –

3. Shadrach, Meshach, and Abednego threw in the fiery furnace – **O KING, WE DO NOT NEED TO DEFEND OURSELVES BEFORE YOU ON THIS MATTER – OUR GOD IS ABLE… - THEY TRUSTED IN GOD AND DEFIED THE KING** – no other God can save this way

4. Nebuchadnezzar's dream of a tree – Daniel interprets the king **WILL GO CRAZY FOR 7 YEARS BECAUSE OF HIS PRIDE** – those who walk in pride he is able to humble

5. Writing on the wall – Nebuchadnezzar's son King Belshazzar gave a banquet for 1000 – he brought out the golden goblets of the temple to use and praised the idols of gold, silver, etc. – hand came out and wrote on the wall King pees on himself – even though he knew of his father's pride and insanity he proceeded to do the same thing – Word's meant you will die and your kingdom will be divided – king slain that night - **KING DARIUS TAKES OVER**

6. King Darius tricked into throwing Daniel into Lion's den – Daniel was not touched - **OTHERS were THROWN IN, AND BEFORE THEY TOUCHED THE GROUND WERE TORN TO PIECES**

7. Daniel dreams of 4 beasts – A lion, bear, leopard, and something terrifying – son of man appears in the dream – 4 beasts are 4 kingdoms – the last kingdom will have one horn that will grow bigger than the previous ones

8. the vision of a ram and a goat – concerns the end of time – seems to be talking about the rise of the Roman Empire – concerns the distant future – I was appalled by the vision. It was beyond understanding

9. **DANIEL'S PRAYER ASKING FOR FORGIVENESS AND MERCY** – we do not make **REQUESTS OF YOU BECAUSE** WE ARE **RIGHTEOUS, BUT BECAUSE OF YOUR GREAT MERCY** – SENT **GABRIEL TO ANSWER PRAYER IMMEDIATELY** (as soon as he began to pray) – **ANSWER SEVENTY SEVENS (490 YEARS) FROM THE ISSUE TO REBUILD UNTIL THE TIME OF CHRIST** – after the 70 7's the anointed one will be cut off – <u>**HE WILL PUT AN END TO SACRIFICE AND OFFERING**</u>

10. Daniel sees the vision of a man – no one else sees it, but it scares him so that the others flee – **THE PERSON (ANGEL) COULDN'T COME FOR 21 DAYS BECAUSE HE WAS DETAINED WITH THE KING OF PERSIA –**

11. The man tells Daniel from the Book of Truth – tells about the kings of the North and South – it seems like there will be a lot of wars and capturing of North and South – vs. 32 with flattery, he will corrupt those who have violated the covenant, **BUT THE PEOPLE WHO KNOW THEIR GOD WILL FIRMLY RESIST HIM** - A king will exalt himself above every god

12. The End times – **MULTITUDES WHO SLEEP IN THE DUST WILL AWAKE, SOME TO EVERLASTING LIFE OTHERS TO SHAME**… - when will the end happen – when the power of the holy people has been finally broken – Many will be purified, made spotless and refined but the wicked will continue to be wicked – **GO YOUR WAY TILL THE END YOU WILL REST, AND THEN AT THE END OF THE DAYS YOU WILL RISE TO RECEIVE YOUR ALLOTTED INHERITANCE**

Hosea

1. **HOSEA MARRIES GOMER HAS 3 CHILDREN**

2. I will not show my love - I will stop their celebrations

3. Hosea told to love his wife - **SO I BOUGHT HER FOR 15 SHEKELS OF SILVER**...

4. Charge against Israel - **US. 6 MY PEOPLE ARE DESTROYED BY LACK OF KNOWLEDGE -** not punish harlots because men consort with shrine prostitutes - even when drinks are gone, they continue their prostitution

5. **SPIRIT OF PROSTITUTION IS IN THEIR HEART** vs. 4 - they will seek help from other kings - God will devour them **- VS. 15 IN THEIR MISERY THEY WILL EARNESTLY SEEK ME.**

6. Lord tore us to pieces but will bind our wounds - let us acknowledge him **- I DESIRE MERCY, NOT SACRIFICE AND ACKNOWLEDGEMENT OF GOD RATHER THAN BURNT OFFERINGS - BANDS OF PRIEST LIE IN AMBUSH**

7. Delight in wickedness and intrigue - **OVER AND OVER GOD SAYS HE LONGS TO REDEEM THEM IF ONLY THEY TURN TO HIM**

8. **THEY SOW THE WIND AND REAP THE WHIRLWIND** vs. 7 - how long will they be incapable of purity - built many altars for sin offerings became altars for sinning

9. Israel is horrible – you love the wages of a prostitute – because your sins are so many, the prophet is considered a fool, the inspired man a maniac – they worship idols and become vile as the thing they loved

10. continued from 9 – as his fruit increased, he built more altars – They make many promises take false oaths, and make agreements; therefore, lawsuits spring up like poisonous weeds in a plowed field – They say to the mountains cover us and to the hills fall on us – Sow for yourselves righteousness reap the fruit of unfailing love … for it is time to seek the Lord until he comes and showers righteousness on you

11. <u>God loves Israel – compares to a small child</u> – It was I who taught Ephraim to walk – My people are determined to turn from me – **MY HEART CHANGED WITHIN ME ALL MY COMPASSION IS AROUSED I WILL NOT CARRY OUT MY FIERCE ANGER …. <u>FOR I AM GOD AND NOT MAN</u>**

12. **SIN OF ISRAEL** – makes a treaty with Assyria and sends olive oil to Egypt – **BUT YOU MUST RETURN TO YOUR GOD; MAINTAIN LOVE AND JUSTICE AND WAIT FOR YOUR GOD ALWAYS.**

13. Sins continued – They offer human sacrifice and kiss the calf-idols – You shall acknowledge no God but me, no savior except me – <u>**WHEN I FED THEM, THEY BECAME SATISFIED WHEN THEY WERE SATISFIED, THEY BECAME PROUD THEN THEY FORGOT ME**</u> – I will ransom them from the grave

14. <u>REPENTANCE BRINGS BLESSINGS</u> – **YOUR SINS HAVE BEEN YOUR DOWNFALL – SAY FORGIVE ALL OUR SINS AND RECEIVE US GRACIOUSLY THAT WE MAY OFFER THE FRUIT OF OUR LIPS** – Assyria cannot save us – we will never again say 'Our gods' – <u>I will heal their waywardness and love them freely</u> – your fruitfulness comes from me – The ways of the Lord are right the righteous walk in them but the rebellious stumble in them

Joel

1. A nation has invaded my land powerful and without number – Repent – Put on sackcloth …. – Declare a holy fast call a sacred assembly – has not your food been cut off before your very eyes (drought and locusts)

2. Army of locusts – before them is Edom behind them a desert – **EVEN NOW RETURN TO ME WITH ALL YOUR HEART WITH FASTING AND WEEPING – REND YOUR HEART NOT YOUR GARMENTS... – DECLARE A HOLY FAST** if you repent God will send grain new wine and oil enough to satisfy you – The day of the Lord – **I WILL POUR OUT MY SPIRIT ON ALL THE PEOPLE YOUR SONS AND DAUGHTERS WILL PROPHESY, YOUR OLD MEN WILL DREAM DREAMS … I WILL SHOW YOU WONDERS …** everyone who calls on the name of the Lord will be saved

3. when I restore the fortunes of Judah and Jerusalem, I will gather all the nations and bring them down … **THEY CAST LOTS FOR MY PEOPLE AND TRADED BOYS FOR PROSTITUTES; THEY SOLD GIRLS FOR WINE... - THEY TOOK MY GOLD AND SILVER FOR THEIR TEMPLES …** - never again will foreigners invade her – Judah inhabited forever and Jerusalem through all generations – their bloodguilt which I have not pardoned I will pardon

Amos

1. Words of Amos 2 years before **EARTHQUAKE** Uzziah king of Judah Jeroboam king of Israel - Judgment against Damascus Tyre Edom Ammon Gaza Moab **Judah**

2. Judgment against Israel - **SELL RIGHTEOUS FOR SILVER NEEDY FOR A PAIR OF SANDALS FATHER SON USE SAME GIRL** - house of God take wine as fines - made Nazarite drink wine commanded prophets not to prophesy

3. Do two walk together unless they have agreed to do so us. 3 - When disaster comes to a city, has not the Lord caused it - ... from the lion's mouth, only 2 legs or a piece of the ear so will the Israelites be saved

4. ****** LOTS OF SINS, SO GOD PUNISHED TO CAUSE HIS PEOPLE TO TURN TO HIM - PREPARE TO MEET YOUR GOD - HE WHO FORMS MOUNTAINS... AND REVEALS HIS THOUGHTS TO MAN**

5. Seek me and live; do not seek ... do not go to... do not journey... seek the Lord and live - you despise him who tells the truth   - a **PRUDENT MAN KEEPS QUIET IN EVIL TIMES** - seek good, not evil so that you may live - day of the lord like man running from a lion only to meet a bear - I hate I despise your religious feasts - away with your music I will not listen to your harps

6. **WOE TO YOU WHO ARE COMPLACENT** - the richest improvise on musical instruments - first to go to exile - I abhor the pride of Jacob rejoice in the conquest of Lo Debar by their own hand

7. Locusts consume the land – Amos pleads to stop so the Lord relented – **TAKES AWAY THE RAIN AND DESTROYS BY FIRE -** Amos pleads to stop so the Lord relented – The Lord raises a plumb line and says everyone to be destroyed by the sword – **AMAZIAH THE PRIEST TRIES TO GET AMOS IN TROUBLE** – not a prophet's son but a Shepard –

8. A basket of ripe fruit – the time is ripe for Israel – in the temple, many, many bodies – flung everywhere! – land will rise and fall like the Nile in Egypt (earthquake) – I will send a famine … **FAMINE OF HEARING THE WORDS OF THE LORD … MEN WILL**

SEARCH FOR THE WORD OF THE LORD, BUT THEY WILL NOT FIND IT

9. Though they _____, I will kill them. Did I not bring Israel from Egypt, Philistines from Caphtor, Arameans from Kir- All the sinners among my people will die by the sword – I then will restore David's fallen tent – never again to be uprooted

Obadiah

Edom descendants of Esau will be completely wiped out – because of your violence against your brother Jacob – don't look down on your brother on the day of his calamity – The day of the lord is near for all nations

Jonah

1. Told to go to Nineveh – Jonah went the other way – on a boat, the seas grew fierce – sleep – **cast lots** and the lot fell to Jonah – told men to throw him over – they refused at first, then they did, and the seas grew calm – whale swallowed Jonah

2. Jonah prays whale vomits him out

3. Preaches to Nineveh – **THEY REPENT**

4. JONAH IS **ANGRY WITH GOD FOR BEING GRACIOUS COMPASSIONATE AND SLOW TO ANGER ABOUNDING IN LOVE** – watches from a distance – vine grows – worm eats – Jonah angry – **GOD SAID YOU ARE MORE CONCERNED WITH A VINE THAN A TOWN WITH 120,000 PEOPLE** and many cattle as well

Micah

1. Micah during the reigns of Jotham, Ahaz, and Hezekiah – the vision concerning Samaria and Jerusalem – Jacob's transgression = Samaria – She gathered her gifts from wages of prostitutes as the wages of prostitutes they will be used again – her wound is incurable it has come to Judah… even to Jerusalem itself – they will go from you to exile

2. Men plan to steal and defraud – God plans to bring disaster to them – You will no longer walk proudly – **FALSE PROPHETS SAY DON'T PROPHESY** – "Is the Spirit of the Lord angry? Does he do such things?" vs. 7 – **I WILL PROPHESY FOR YOU PLENTY OF WINE AND BEER, THAT IS JUST WHAT THE PEOPLE WANT TO HEAR** – Deliverance promised

3. Leaders rebuked – you tear people apart then cry out to the Lord, but he will not answer because of the evil they have done – leaders judge for a bribe – **PRIESTS TEACH FOR A PRICE – PROPHETS TELL FORTUNES FOR MONEY** – then they say the Lord is among us no disaster will come upon us

4. In the last days – many will come and say … Teach us… The law will go out from Zion the word of the lord from Jerusalem – Every man will sit under his own vine – no one will make them afraid – **ALL THE NATIONS MAY WALK IN THE NAME OF THEIR GODS WE WILL WALK IN THE NAME OF THE LORD – THEY DO NOT KNOW THE THOUGHTS OF THE LORD THEY DO NOT UNDERSTAND HIS PLAN**

5. But you, Bethlehem… out of you will come for me one who will be ruler over Israel whose origins are from old from ancient times – his greatness will reach the ends of the earth, and he will be their peace – I will destroy witchcraft – you will no longer bow down to the work of your hands

6. My people, what have I done to you? How have I burdened you? I brought you out of Egypt … - **NO SACRIFICES WILL PLEASE GOD EXCEPT "THAT YOU ACT JUSTLY AND TO LOVE MERCY AND TO WALK HUMBLY WITH YOUR GOD"** – Her rich men are violent –

7. Godly have been swept from the land, not one upright man remains –
a man's enemies are the members of his own household - But as for
me, I watch in hope for the Lord, I wait for the God my Savior; my
God will hear me. – Because I have sinned against him, I will bear
the Lord's wrath… He will bring me out into the light. I will see his
righteousness – As in the days when you came out of Egypt, I will
show them my wonders – **WHO IS A GOD LIKE YOU WHO
PARDONS SIN AND FORGIVES TRANSGRESSIONS… YOU
DO NOT STAY ANGRY FOREVER BUT DELIGHT TO
SHOW COMPASSION.**

Nahum

1. Oracle concerning Nineveh - the lord is angry with Nineveh - clouds are the dust of his feet. He rebukes the sea and dries it up **- HE CARES FOR THOSE WHO TRUST HIM** - I will release Judah from you

2. Nineveh to fall

3. Woe to the city of blood - you have increased the number of your merchants

Habakkuk

1. ? How long must I call for help, but you do not listen – Why do you tolerate wrong? – I am raising the Babylonians – Second complaint – Why do you tolerate the treacherous?

2. The righteous will live by his faith – **WOE TO HIM WHO PILES UP STOLEN GOODS** – Woe to him who builds his realm by unjust gain – Woe to him who builds a city with bloodshed – **THE EARTH WILL BE FILLED WITH THE KNOWLEDGE OF THE GLORY OF THE LORD** – Woe to him who gets his neighbor drunk so that he can gaze on his naked bodies – - the destruction of animals will terrify you – Woe to him who speaks to wood "come to life" – vs. 20 **"BUT THE LORD IS IN HIS HOLY TEMPLE LET ALL THE EARTH BE SILENT BEFORE HIM."**

3. Habakkuk's prayer – decay crept into my bones

Zephaniah

1. During the reign of Josiah king of Judah – Against Judah – those who turn back from following the Lord and neither seek the Lord nor inquire of him vs. 6 – **THE LORD HAS PREPARED A SACRIFICE**; he has consecrated those he has invited on the day of the Lord's sacrifice vs. 7-8 – **PUNISH THOSE WHO ARE COMPLACENT WHO THINK THE LORD WILL DO NOTHING EITHER GOOD OR BAD** – neither their silver nor gold will save them – the whole world will be consumed

2. Seek the lord all you humble of the land you who do what he commands seek righteousness seek humility perhaps you will be sheltered – Philistia – I will destroy you, and none will be left – Moab and Ammon – will become like Sodom and Gomorrah – the remnant will plunder you – Cushites will be slain – Assyria and Nineveh will be destroyed

3. **JERUSALEM – PROPHETS ARE ARROGANT – PRIESTS PROFANE THE SANCTUARY** – unrighteous Know no shame – to the city "<u>**SURELY YOU WILL FEAR ME AND ACCEPT CORRECTION**</u>" **– BUT STILL EAGER TO ACT CORRUPTLY** – the whole world will be consumed – **I WILL REMOVE FROM THE CITY THOSE WHO REJOICE IN THEIR PRIDE – BUT I WILL LEAVE… THE MEEK AND HUMBLE WHO TRUST IN THE NAME OF THE LORD** – He will take great delight in you; <u>he will quiet you with love;</u> he will rejoice over you with singing

Haggai

1. The second year of King Darius – is it not time to build the lord's house – the people are building their own paneled houses – barely making a living – Why? **BECAUSE OF MY HOUSE REMAINS A RUIN – <u>I CALLED FOR A DROUGHT… TO MAKE YOU TURN TO ME</u>** – remnant heard the message feared the Lord and started rebuilding –

2. Has anyone seen the temple in its former glory – does it seem like nothing? – **THE GLORY OF THE PRESENT WILL BE GREATER THAN THE FORMER TEMPLE** – From this day forward, I will bless you – Zerubbabel, I will make you my signet ring

Zechariah

1. In the second year of Darius - **RETURN TO ME, AND I WILL RETURN TO YOU** – Then they repented – vision of man among trees with horses – 70 years are over and Israel to be restored – 4 horns that scattered Judah… 4 craftsmen to take them apart

2. The vision of a man with a measuring stick – to measure Jerusalem – a city without a wall because of the large number of people and livestock – the lord will be the wall – shout and be glad – Be still before the Lord

3. **VISION OF ANGEL OF THE LORD, SATAN AND HIGH PRIEST** (Joshua) in filthy garments – given new clothes to show will forgive sins – I will give you peace among those standing here – remove sin on a single day

4. a vision of a gold lampstand, two olive trees also, 2 olive branches, and 2 golden pipes that pour golden oil

5. Flying scroll – says on one side every thief will be banished other side everyone who swears falsely will be banished – woman in basket wicked taken to Babylonia

6. vision 4 chariots – 4 spirits of the heaven – they were sent throughout the earth – **ZECHARIAH TOLD TO MAKE A CROWN FOR JOSHUA THE HIGH PRIEST AND PLACE IT ON HIM – TOLD HE WOULD RULE AS HIGH PRIEST** – then those who are far away will come to help build the temple – this will happen if you diligently obey the Lord

7. Should I continue to mourn and fast as I have on the fifth and seventh month as I have the last 70 years? **ADMINISTER TRUE JUSTICE SHOW MERCY AND COMPASSION TO ONE ANOTHER – DO NOT OPPRESS THE WIDOW, FATHERLESS, ALIEN OF THE POOR** – in your hearts do not think evil of each other – "**WHEN I CALLED, THEY DID NOT LISTEN; SO, WHEN THEY CALLED, I WOULD NOT LISTEN," SAYS THE LORD ALMIGHTY VS. 13**

8. blessings for Jerusalem – **I AM VERY JEALOUS FOR JERUSALEM** – I will save my people from the east and the west… - I will not deal with the remnant as I did in the past - **I WILL**

DWELL IN JERUSALEM AGAIN – THINGS YOU ARE TO DO - SPEAK THE TRUTH, RENDERS SOUND JUDGMENT – DO NOT PLOT EVIL – DO NOT LOVE TO SWEAR FALSELY – fasts of the 4th 5th 7th and 10th months to become joyful – people will seek advice from the lord in Jerusalem – 10 men will grab one Jew and say Let us go with you because we heard that God is with you

9. Oracle against Israel's enemies – Coming of the King – **VS. 9 YOUR KING COMES TO YOU RIGHTEOUS AND HAVING SALVATION, GENTLE AND RIDING ON A DONKEY** – the lord will appear

10. Ask the Lord for rain in the springtime; **IT IS THE LORD WHO MAKES THE STORM CLOUDS** – From Judah will come to the cornerstone … the tent peg… the battle bow… every ruler. – **THEY WILL BE AS THOUGH I HAD NOT REJECTED THEM –**

11. 2 shepherds – replaced 3 shepherds in one month – took staff called Favor and broke it **REVOKING THE COVENANT BETWEEN GOD AND THE NATIONS – PAID 30 PIECES OF SILVER** – took the silver and threw it into the house of the Lord to the potter – then I broke my second staff called union **BREAKING THE BROTHERHOOD BETWEEN JUDAH AND ISRAEL**

12. The Lord who stretches the heavens, who lays the foundation of the earth, and who forms the spirit of man within him – The Lord will save the dwellings of Judah first… - **VS.10 AND I WILL POUR OUT ON THE HOUSE OF DAVID AND THE INHABITANTS OF JERUSALEM A SPIRIT OF GRACE AND SUPPLICATION. THEY WILL LOOK ON ME, THE ONE THEY HAVE PIERCED, AND THEY WILL MOURN FOR HIM AS ONE MOURNS FOR AN ONLY CHILD…**

13. **ON THAT DAY, A FOUNTAIN WILL BE OPENED TO THE HOUSE OF DAVID AND THE INHABITANTS OF JERUSALEM TO CLEANSE THEM FROM SIN AND IMPURITY – I WILL REMOVE BOTH THE PROPHETS AND THE SPIRIT OF IMPURITY FROM THE LAND** – 2/3 struck down and perish remainder to be refined and tested

14. **ON THAT DAY, HIS FEET WILL STAND ON THE MOUNT OF OLIVES – ON THAT DAY, THERE WILL BE NO LIGHT… WHEN EVENING COMES, THERE WILL BE**

LIGHT – ON THAT DAY, LIVING WATER WILL FLOW OUT FROM JERUSALEM – THE LORD WILL BE KING OVER THE WHOLE EARTH – big plague – survivors to go to Jerusalem and celebrate the feast of Tabernacles every year – Every pot in Jerusalem and Judah will be holy

Malachi

1. Jacob, I loved, but Esau I hated – I destroyed Edom's houses when they rebuild, I will destroy again – Shown contempt to the Lord by placing defiled food on memy alter – brought blind and crippled animals – **YOU SAY WHAT A BURDEN OF THE SACRIFICES** – cursed is the cheat who vows to give one animal and then gives a blemished one instead

2. **FOR THE LIPS OF THE PRIEST OUGHT TO PRESERVE KNOWLEDGE AND FROM HIS MOUTH MEN SHOULD SEEK INSTRUCTION BECAUSE HE IS A MESSENGER OF GOD – BUT YOUR TEACHING CAUSES MANY TO STUMBLE** – Have we, not all one Father – Judah has broken faith – **I HATE DIVORCE** – Has not the lord made them one? In flesh and spirit, they are his – why one? Because he was seeking godly offspring

3. I will send my messenger who will prepare the way before me – Who can stand when he appears – then the Lord will have men who will bring offerings in righteousness – I will be quick to testify against sorcerers, adulteress… - Robbing God – **test me** in this – you have said it is futile to serve the Lord the wicked are prosperous, etc. **– YOU WILL AGAIN SEE THE DISTINCTION BETWEEN THE RIGHTEOUS AND THE WICKED**

4. Surely the Day is coming – **I WILL SEND THE PROPHET ELIJAH BEFORE THAT GREAT AND DREADFUL DAY OF THE LORD COMES** – he will turn father to children and children to their fathers, or I will come and strike a curse

New Testament

Matthew

1. Genealogy of Jesus –14 generations from Abraham to David, 14 from David to Exile, 14 from exile to Jesus - Birth of Jesus

2. visit of the wise men – Herod called together all the chief priests and teachers and asked them where the Christ was to be born, and they said Bethlehem – escaped to Egypt and returned to and settled in Nazareth – 4 references to OT scriptures

3. John the Baptist – dresses exactly like Elijah – Baptism of Jesus

4. Temptation of Jesus – devil left him, and angels came and attended him – Jesus begins to preach, "Repent for the kingdom of heaven is near" – Calls first disciples – Jesus heals the very sick

5. Beatitudes – **BLESSED ARE YOU WHEN PEOPLE INSULT YOU BECAUSE OF ME …. BECAUSE IN THE SAME WAY THEY PERSECUTED THE PROPHETS** … - You are the Salt… you are the light… A city on a hill – has come to fulfilt the law – your righteousness needs to surpass the Pharisees – if you have something against your brother, then leave the alter make peace, then offer your sacrifice – Adultery – Divorce – do not swear at all – turn your cheek – give to anyone that asks – love your enemies – **BE PERFECT, THEREFORE, AS YOUR HEAVENLY FATHER IS PERFECT**

6. **GIVE IN SECRET – PRAY IN SECRET** – forgive and you will be forgiven – **FAST IN SECRET** – No one can serve two masters – can't serve God and money – Do not worry – seek first the kingdom of heaven and all these things will be given to you as well

7. Do not judge others rashly – ask, seek knock – in everything do to others as you would have them do to you – Narrow and wide gates - watch out for false prophets – not everyone who says to me "Lord" will enter the kingdom – **EVERY ONE WHO HEARS THE WORD AND PUTS THEM INTO PRACTICE IS LIKE THE WISE MAN WHO BUILT HIS HOUSE ON A ROCK**

8. Man with Leprosy – if you are willing, you can make me clean – I am willing – Faith of the centurion – Lord, I do not deserve to have you come to my house say the word… **JESUS WAS AMAZED** – many will come from the east and the west – Jesus heals Peter's mother-in-law – heals many – drives out spirits with a word – the cost of following Jesus – Jesus calms the storm - even the winds and waves obey him – healed two, demon-possessed men went into pigs and died – town people pleaded for him to leave

9. Healed the paralytic – crowed saw filled with awe and praised god who gave authority to men – calling of Matthew – eats with sinners – healthy don't need a doctor – fasting when Jesus leaves then they will fast – raised a girl from the dead – healed the woman who was bleeding – according to your faith heals blind and mute – **NOTHING LIKE THIS HAS EVER BEEN SEEN IN ISRAEL** – Pharisees say by the prince of demons he does this – harvest is plentiful workers are few

10. Jesus sends out the 12 – gave authority heal everything – do not go to the Gentiles – don't take money or provisions the worker is worth his keep – I am sending you among wolves – **BE AS SHREWD AS SNAKES AND AS INNOCENT AS DOVES** – be on guard against men – when arrested don't worry about what to say it won't be you speaking but the spirit of your Father speaking through you – when persecuted flee – do not be afraid of them – do not be afraid of those who kill the body… rather the one who can destroy both soul and the body – whoever acknowledges me before men… - **I DID NOT COME TO BRING PEACE BUT THE SWORD** – anyone who loves his father or mother more than me … - <u>whoever finds his life will lose it…</u>

11. Among those born of women, there has not risen anyone greater than John the Baptist – <u>**If you are willing to accept it, he is the Elijah who was to come – s**</u>ome say John neither ate nor drank, but the son of man came eating and drinking **BUT WISDOM IS PROVED RIGHT BY HER ACTIONS** – Jesus began to denounce the cities in which most of the miracles were performed – come to me all who are weary and burdened and I will give you rest… for I am gentle and humble in heart

12. Jesus heals on the Sabbath – when questioned says, "<u>If you had known what these words mean, 'I desire mercy not sacrifice,' you would not condemn the innocent</u> – **QUOTES ISAIAH AND SAYS**

'HERE IS MY SERVANT' – crowds say could this be the son of David? – enter a strong man's house – anyone who speaks against the Holy Spirit will not be forgiven – out of the overflow of the heart the mouth speaks – **what you dwell on comes out in your actions –** Pharisees ask for a sign – Jesus says he will be 3 days and 3 nights in the earth – the sign of Jonah – evil spirit leaves you comes back and finds it swept clean then comes back with seven more spirits and makes it worse – whoever does the will of my Father in heaven is my brother and sister and mother

13. Parable of the Sower – spoke in parables as prophesized by Isaiah – Many prophets and righteous men longed to see what you see… worries of this life and deceitfulness of wealth choke it – the parable of weeds, mustard seed, and yeast – he did not say anything to the crowds without using parables – Parable explained – harvest is the end of the age, and harvesters are angels – angels will separate the wicked from the righteous – prophet without honor in his hometown

14. John the Baptist beheaded – Herod thinks Jesus is John the Baptist risen from the dead – feeds 5000 –Walks on water – when crossed over, people beg to touch his garment to be healed; they do and are

15. What comes out of his mouth, that is what makes him 'unclean' – they are blind guides, the blind leading the blind both will fall in a pit – the faith of a Canaanite woman "but even the dogs eat the crumbs that fall from their masters' table – feeds the 4000 after they had nothing to eat for 3 days by being with him

16. demand for a sign - yeast of the Pharisees - peters confession that Jesus is the Christ - Jesus tells them plainly that he must die - whoever wants to save his life will lose it.... - gains the whole world yet forfeit his soul ...,

17. Transfiguration - Moses Elijah Jesus - disciples couldn't heal a boy because of little faith - money in the fishes mouth for taxes

18. little ones greatest in heaven - don't cause little ones to sin - **WOE TO THE WORLD BECAUSE OF THE THINGS THAT CAUSE PEOPLE TO SIN** - their angels in heaven watch little ones - a brother who sins against you - 2 ask you will receive - **FORGIVE FROM HEART**

19. divorce - little children brought to Jesus for him to place hands on them and pray for them - rich man - to be perfect, sell possessions

and give to the poor - everyone who leaves stuff for my sake will receive 100 times more

20. Parable of the workers in the vineyard – I am not being unfair to you… Don't I have the right to do what I want with my own money? – Jesus again predicts his death – Mother comes wanting her sons to be at Jesus's right and left – whoever wants to be great must be your servant – blind men healed and follow Jesus

21. Triumphal Entry – When Jesus entered Jerusalem, the whole city stirred and asked who is this – Jesus overturned the tables – From the lips of children and infants you have ordained praise – fig tree – if you believe you will receive whatever you ask – John's baptism wheredid it come from – then I (Jesus) will not answer you where my authority is from – parable 2 sons one said I won't but did it the other… - the parable of the tenants of the winery killed the son – **KINGDOM OF GOD TAKEN FROM YOU AND GIVEN TO A PEOPLE THAT WILL PRODUCE FRUIT**

22. Parable of the wedding banquet – paid no attention to the King and even mistreated and killed his servants – many are invited, but few are chosen – Taxes to Caesar – Pharisees try to trap Jesus – Give to Caesar what is Caesar's – Marriage at the resurrection – "**YOU ARE IN ERROR BECAUSE YOU DO NOT KNOW THE SCRIPTURES OR THE POWER OF GOD**" – they will be like the angels in heaven – "**HE IS NOT THE GOD OF THE DEAD BUT OF THE LIVING**" – Greatest command – whose son is the Christ?

23. Seven Woes – they do not practice what they teach – everything they do is done for men to see – do not call anyone on earth father or teacher – whoever exalts himself will be humbled… woe to you teachers of the law you shut the kingdom of heaven in Men's faces – woe… you travel over land and sea to make a single convert, then make him twice the son of hell as you are – woe… swear by the temple must swear by the gold of the temple – woe… **give a tenth of everything but neglect the more important matters of justice, mercy, and faithfulness –** woe… wipe the outside of the dish but inside is full of greed and self-indulgence – woe… you are whitewashed tombs outside, nice inside full of bones – woe… if we lived in the time of the prophets…you snakes, how will you escape being condemned to hell? – Jerusalem, you who kill the prophets and stone those sent to you…

24. Signs of the end of the age – I tell you the truth, not one stone here will be left on another – you will be handed over to be persecuted – because of the increase in wickedness, the love of most will grow cold – this generation will not pass until all these things have happened – son of man will come at an hour when you do not expect him

25. Parables – ten virgins – keep watch because you do not know the hour or the day I will come – talents – everyone that has will be given more, and he will have an abundance – sheep, and goats – **DUEDO TO THE LEAST YOU DO FOR ME** – they will go away to eternal punishment or eternal life – depart from me those cursed into the eternal fire

26. **AS YOU KNOW, THE PASSOVER IS IN TWO DAYS. I WILL BE CRUCIFIED – WE NEED TO KILL HIM BUT NOT DURING THE PASSOVER** – woman breaks the alabaster jar and anoints Jesus – Judas agrees to betray Jesus 30 pcs. Of silver – Lord's supper – this is the blood of the covenant that is poured out for many for the forgiveness of sin – I will strike the shepherd and the sheep will be scattered – prayer on Gethsemane – My soul is overwhelmed with sorrow – spirit willing but the body is weak – went away once more and prayed the same thing – Jesus arrested – do you think I could call angels to help but then how will the scriptures be fulfilled – all taking place that the writings of the prophets might be fulfilled – before the Sanhedrin – **HIGH PRIEST TORE HIS CLOTHES SPIT IN HIS FACE AND STRUCK HIM** – peter disowns Jesus

27. Judas hangs himself – the priests take the blood money and buy the potter's field – Pilate "Are you the king of the Jews? Yes – washed hands and sent Jesus to be crucified – soldiers mocked him and struck him on the head – robbers insulted him – Jesus cried out and gave up his spirit – people rose from the dead and after Jesus's resurrection went into town – curtain toretornin two – the burial of Jesus – guards sent to the tomb – **CHIEF PRIESTS WE REMEMBER HE SAID HE WOULD RAISE HIMSELF FROM THE DEAD** –

28. Resurrection women see him first – great commission – go out and baptize in the name of the Father, the Son, the Holy Spirit and obey my teachings

Mark

1. John the Baptist came preaching baptism for repentance for the forgiveness of sins - confessing they were baptized - wore camel hair - baptism and temptation - he was with the wild animals and angels attended him - Jesus preached repent and believe - **SPIRIT SAYS YOU ARE THE HOLY ONE OF GOD** - Jesus heals many - very early goes out to solitary place - <u>man healed told not to tell of healing as a result could no longer enter a town</u>

2. Jesus heals paralytic - through the roof - calling of Levi - Jesus eats with sinners - not come to call the righteous but sinners - fasting - <u>the Sabbath was made for man, not man for the Sabbath</u>

3. healing on Sabbath Pharisees would not answer "he looked around in **ANGER AND DEEPLY DISTRESSED AT THEIR STUBBORN HEARTS"** - spirits call him the son of god - appointed the 12 - **JESUS FAMILY THOUGHT HE WAS OUT OF HIS MIND** - a house divided - blasphemes against the holy spirit like tying up strong man to rob him

4. parable of the seeds - lamp on a stand - growing seed, **KINGDOM OF GOD LIKE PLANT NIGHT AND DAY GROWS, BUT MAN DOES NOT KNOW HOW** - parable mustard seed - Jesus calms storm even wind and waves obey him

5. Healed a man named Legion into 2000 pigs – he was very strong and broke chains and leg irons – asked to follow Jesus, but Jesus told him to stay and tell his town what was done for him – sick woman healed by touching Jesus after 12 years – synagogue ruler asks Jesus to heal his daughter – he raises her back to life

6. **AT HIS HOMETOWN, HE COULD NOT DO ANY MIRACLES EXCEPT HEAL A FEW PEOPLE – <u>HE WAS AMAZED AT THEIR LACK OF FAITH</u>** – sent out the twelve – preached repent – performed many miracles – King Herod heard about this – <u>thought John had been raised from the dead – some thought he was Elijah others a prophet from long ago</u> – Herodias nursed a grudge against John the Baptist – <u>Herod heard John he was puzzled yet he liked to listen to him</u> – Jesus feeds the 5000

7. holding to tradition, the Pharisees asked why the men ate with unclean hands – Jesus quotes Isaiah – **out of you is what makes you unclean – not what goes in you – in saying this, Jesus declared all foods clean –** crumbs for a foreign woman – healed a def man – told not to tell but the more he told not to the more they did –

8. Feed the 4,000 – He sighed deeply to rebuke the Pharisees – talking to the disciples, Jesus asks are your hearts hardened – **JESUS LAYS HIS HANDS ON A MAN TWICE TO HEAL HIM** – Pete's confession – Jesus tells them plainly that he must die and be raised again – save your life must lose it – ashamed of me I am ashamed of you

9. Transfiguration - Elijah Moses - evil spirit boy - **Father help me overcome my unbelief** - I must die, did not understand **what rising from the dead meant -** greatest - whoever for us not against us - cause little ones to sin

10. Divorce – Little children, Jesus took little children in his arms and blessed them – rich young man fell on his knees to ask Jesus – you will receive 100 times as much in this present age – Jesus predicts his death again – James and John request to sit at his right hand – first will be last… - Go your faith has healed you to a blind man

11. Triumphal entry – good account of the fig tree that Jesus cursed – by what authority? Answer me by what authority did John have? Everyone held that John really was a prophet

12. parable of the tenants he sent his son last of all – the Pharisees knew this was a parable against them – Give to Caesar what is Caesar's – marriage at the resurrection – **I AM THE GOD OF ABRAHAM… HE IS NOT THE GOD OF THE DEAD BUT THE LIVING.** – Greatest commandment Love your God… this is more important than all burnt offerings and sacrifices – the widow gives all she has

13. Signs of the end of the age – Mount of olives opposite the temple – the gospel must first be preached to all the nations – If the days had not been cut short, no one would survive – this generation will not pass until all these things have passed – day and hour unknown – I say to everyone Watch!

14. two days before Jesus's arrest, they plotted to kill him but said not during the Feast because the people would riot – she poured perfume on his body to prepare for his burial – Judas told the Pharisees, and they were pleased – Lord's Supper – Jesus predicts Peter's denial –

Gethsemane – Jesus arrested – Judas kisses him – <u>everyone flees –
young man flees naked –</u> before the Sanhedrin – Jesus silent in front
of false accusers, then asked Are you the Christ, the son of the
Blessed One? **I AM,** - Peter disowns Jesus with curses

15. Jesus before Pilate – are you the king of the Jews? **YES** – crucifixion
– the death of Jesus – tore the curtain from top to bottom –
Arimathea member of the council buries Christ, he was also waiting
for the kingdom to come

16. On the first day of the week, Jesus arose – the Marys were the first to
see him – disciples were told but did not believe – Jesus rebuked
them for their unbelief – vs. 16:16 Whoever believes and is baptized
– disciples confirmed his word by signs that accompanied it

Luke

1. A priest named Zechariah and his wife Elizabeth **BOTH OF THE LINE OF AARON GIVE BIRTH TO JOHN** – Angel comes to Zechariah – **because doubted was made mute until the 8th day of the birth –** Never to have wine – John to bring back many to the Lord – In Nazareth Mary told of pregnancy – vs. 37 for nothing is impossible with God – Mary spends 3 months with Elizabeth – Mary's song

2. Birth of Jesus – shepherds and angels – the great company of angels appear to the shepherds – 2 times it says Mary treasured up all these things and pondered them in her heart – Jesus presented at the temple **– 2 PEOPLE WAITING TO SEE THE GLORY OF THE LORD SEE JESUS** – Jesus left behind at the temple –

3. John preaches repentance and baptism – if you have two coats, give to one with none – **give food to the needy** – don't extort live on what you earn – I am not the Christ he will baptize with the holy spirit and fire – Jesus's baptism – genealogy traced through Mary to Adam and God

4. Temptation of Christ – Do not put god to the test – Jesus reads at Nazareth, "Today the scripture is fulfilled you are hearing" – **THEY TRIED TO THROW HIM OFF A CLIFF – ONLY LEPER HEALED IN OT WAS NOT A JEW ONLY WIDOW THAT WAS GIVEN SPECIAL TREATMENT WAS NOT EITHER –** evil spirits call Jesus the Holy One of God! – Jesus heals many – asks to stay, and says I must preach the good news to other towns; that is why I am here

5. the calling of Peter, James, and John – after talking to the crowd, Jesus tells **PETER TO GO OUT AND LOWER THEIR NETS. THEY CATCH SO LARGE IT BEGINS TO SINK TWO BOATS** – left everything to follow Jesus – Heals a Leper – Heals a paralytic that was lowered through the roof – Get up your sins are forgiven – calling of Levi – I have not come to call the righteous but sinners to repentance – after Jesus is taken, then they will fast – **PARABLE OF THE WINESKINS**

6. teachings of Jesus – Lord of the Sabbath – restores a man and makes the Pharisees furious – spends the night praying and then picks the

twelve – blessings and woes – Blessed are you when men hate you … **EXCLUDE YOU AND INSULT YOU AND REJECT YOU AS EVIL BECAUSE OF THE SON OF MAN – LOVE YOUR ENEMIES** – if you love those who love you everyone does that – do not judge… do not condemn… forgive… give – tree and it's fruit – why call me lord and not do what I say

7. faith of the centurion - built synagogue for them - **SAY WORD AND SERVANT HEALED - JESUS TOUCHES A COFFIN AND RAISES A WIDOW'S SON** - Jesus and John the Baptist

8. Jesus traveled accompanied by the 12, and a number of women who supported him – Parable of the seed – Lamp stand – consider carefully how you listen – Jesus' mother and brothers are those who hear and put into practice – Calms the storm – **WINDS AND WAVES OBEY HIM** – healing of Legion – told not to go with Jesus but to go to town and tell what was done – Jesus heals the woman from bleeding and **RAISES THE SYNAGOGUE LEADER, JAIRUS' DAUGHTER FROM THE DEAD**

9. Jesus sends out the 12 – **HEROD THINKS JESUS IS JOHN THE BAPTIST AND TRIED TO SEE HIM** – feeds the 5000 – Peter's confession – If anyone would come after me he must deny himself and take up his cross daily and follow me – transfiguration – **DISCIPLES CAN'T HEAL A BOY JESUS DOES** – told the 12 about his upcoming death and they did not grasp it and were afraid to ask him – the greatest – Samaritan town refuses Jesus – James and John want to call down fire from heaven – the cost of following Jesus

10. **JESUS SENDS OUT THE 72** – many instructions, including **eat and drink whatever they give you** – woe to many cities because they do not believe – I will give you the ability to overcome the power of the enemy – **Jesus full of Joy praised God** for showing these things to little ones instead the wise and learned – Good Samaritan – the one who had mercy on him was the good man – Mary doesn't help Martha but instead listens to Jesus

11. How to pray – **ASK IN BOLDNESS, AND YOU WILL RECEIVE** – ask, seek, knock – Jesus and Beelzebub – kingdom divided can't stand someone great has come which means the kingdom of God has come – Evil leaves a person comes back with 7 others – Blessed are those who hear and obey the word – one greater than Solomon is here – the sign of Jonah – Lamp and the Body – Six

Woes – Jesus did not wash before eating – **you neglect justice and the love of God –** you load people down with burdens and don't lift a finger to help them - you have taken away the key to knowledge

12. warnings and encouragement – do not fear the man who can kill the body but fear him who has the power to throw you into hell, **Yes I tell you to fear him** – rich fool – be on guard against all kinds of greed – do not store up for yourself and not be rich toward God – do not worry – **life is more than food** – do not set your heart on what you will eat or drink – sell your possessions and give to the poor – be ready for his return – bring not peace but division – interpret the times

13. **Repent or perish – 18 who died when a wall fell are they guiltier than all living, NO! unless you repent you will perish –** cripple woman healed on the Sabbath – all his opponents were humiliated – Kingdom like a mustard seed – Narrow door – sorrow for Jerusalem – no prophet can die outside Jerusalem

14. Invited to a banquet, take the least seat, then you will be honored when they ask you to move up – the parable of the great banquet – the cost of following – hate your father, mother, wife, etc., carry your cross and follow me – **GIVE UP EVERYTHING OR YOU CAN NOT BE MY DISCIPLE**

15. Lost and Found – Parables Lost Sheep – lost coin – lost son

16. Shrewd manager – use your worldly wealth to gain friends for yourselves so that when it is gone, you will be welcomed into eternal dwellings – **THE LAW AND THE PROPHETS WERE PROCLAIMED UNTIL JOHN. SINCE THAT TIME, THE GOOD NEWS OF THE KINGDOM OF GOD IS BEING PREACHED** – rich man and Lazarus – If they do not listen to Moses and the prophets, they will not be convinced even if someone rises from the dead

17. do not cause a little one to sin – forgive every time someone asks – small faith is all you need to do great things – **we are unworthy servants; we have only done our duty** – ten healed one comes back and thanks Jesus – **DON'T LOOK FOR THE KINGDOM BECAUSE THE KINGDOM OF GOD IS WITHIN YOU** – whoever tries to keep his life will lose it….

18. A parable to show them **that they should always pray and not give up –** the parable of the persistent widow – the parable of the tax

collect – to some who were confident of their own righteousness and looked down on – babies brought to Jesus – the rich ruler <u>– Jesus predicts his death – the disciples did not understand any of this –</u> a blind beggar receives his sight

19. Zacchaeus – I give half to the poor and anyone that I have wronged I will pay back 4 times – Parable of the ten minas – **TO WHOM THAT HAS MORE WILL BE GIVEN** – the Triumphal entry – Jesus wept over Jerusalem –**TELLS OF FUTURE DESTRUCTION** – Jesus drives out the money changers

20. by what authority do you do this – by what authority did John do things, man or god – Parable of the tenants, Pharisees thought he was speaking against them – <u>spies try to trap Jesus</u> – do we need to pay taxes – what about marriage in the resurrection – Jesus asked whose son the Christ is –

21. the widow's offering – the end of the age – **TEMPLE TO BE DESTROYED – WHEN – WHEN ARMIES SURROUND JERUSALEM –** the end when Jesus comes coming in a cloud – <u>nations will be perplexed by the roaring and tossing of the sea – be careful, or your hearts will be weighed down with dissipation, drunkenness and the anxieties of life</u>

22. Satan entered Judas, and he met with the Pharisees – Last supper – I have eagerly desired to eat this Passover with you before I suffer – do this in remembrance of me – I confer on you a kingdom – <u>Simon Satan has asked to sift you</u> – **I TOLD YOU NOT TO TAKE ANYTHING NOW I TELL YOU TAKE A PURSE AND SELL YOUR TUNIC TO BUY A SWORD** – Jesus prays on the mount of olives – men fall asleep from exhaustion – sweat was like drops of blood – Jesus betrayed and arrested – Peter disowns Christ – Guards mock Jesus – Jesus before the council – **ARE YOU THE SON OF GOD – YOU ARE RIGHT IN SAYING I AM**

23. are you the king of the Jews - **yes** - Herod and soldiers ridiculed Jesus - Barabas was released he had committed murder and insurrection - **OTHER CRIMINAL CRUCIFIED ASKS JESUS TO REMEMBER HIM** - didn't come on Saturday to the grave because obedient to the commandment

24. Resurrection - women find the tomb empty, others don't believe - Jesus appears to many - explains OT to them - eats fish

John

1. In the beginning....- **HE OWNED THE WORLD, BUT THE WORLD DID NOT RECOGNIZE HIM** – to those who receive Him, **HE GAVE THE RIGHT TO BECOME CHILDREN OF GOD** – Law through Moses – grace and truth through Jesus – John the Baptist says he is not the Christ – I baptize with water – Jesus the lamb of god – he will baptize with the Holy Spirit – calling of Phillip and Nathanael

2. water to wine – clears the temple – what authority – destroy the temple I will raise it in three days – He did not need man's testimony about man for he knew what was in a man

3. Jesus teaches Nicodemus – you must be born again – No one has ever gone into heaven except the one who came from heaven – whoever lives by the truth comes into the light – he spent time with them baptizing – people constantly came to John to be baptized – **THE OTHER ONE IS BAPTIZING, AND EVERY ONE IS GOING TO HIM** – I must become less and he more – whoever believes in the Son has eternal life

4. Jesus talks to the Samaritan woman – Jesus's disciples were baptizing – Sir, give me this water so that I won't have to keep coming to draw water – you will worship not on this mountain or in Jerusalem – God is spirit – worship in spirit - - **I KNOW THE MESSIAH IS COMING – I WHO SPEAK TO YOU AM HE** – I have food to eat that you know nothing of – my food is to do the will of the one who sent me – many Samaritans believe – we know that this man really is the Savior of the world – Jesus heals an official's son

5. **38-YEAR-OLD HEALED BY JESUS** – didn't know who Jesus was – later when he found out, he told the Pharisees – **NOT ONLY WAS HE BREAKING THE SABBATH, HE WAS CLAIMING THAT GOD WAS HIS FATHER MAKING HIM EQUAL** – the father loves the son and shows him all he does – all judgment to the son – time is coming when all in graves will hear his voice – my judgment is just – If I testify about myself my testimony is not valid (John testified about me) – **you study the scriptures because you think by them you have eternal life** – how can you believe if you

accept praise from one another – Your accuser is Moses on whom you have set your hope – but since you do not believe what he wrote how can you

6. believe what I say?

7. Feed 5000 – asked Phillip where shall we buy food – Andrew answered - here are 5 loaves and 2 fish – He withdrew because the crowd intended to make him king by force – walks on water – boat 3 miles out – crowd finds Jesus – <u>you are looking for me not because you saw miracles but because your stomachs were filled</u> – **work of god is this; to believe in the one he has sent** – **THE BREAD OF GOD IS HE WHO COMES DOWN FROM HEAVEN AND GIVES LIFE TO THE WORLD - - I AM THE BREAD OF LIFE** – the will of one who sent me I shall lose none of all the that he has given me – **NO ONE CAN COME TO ME UNLESS THE WHO SENT ME DRAWS HIM** – no one has seen the father except the one who is from God – I am the bread of life – this bread is my flesh – unless you eat my flesh and drink my blood you have no life in him – many desert Jesus – does this offend you – words I have spoken to you are spirit and they are life – **MANY DESERTED AND ONE WOULD BETRAY HIM THAT IS WHY HE SAID THAT NO ONE CAN COME TO ME UNLESS THE FATHER ENABLED HIM** – do you want to leave too – you have the words to eternal life

8. Jesus secretly goes to the feast of Tabernacles – in the middle of the feast, Jesus starts teaching – **YOU CIRCUMCISE ON THE SABBATH. WHY ARE YOU ANGRY WHEN I HEAL THE WHOLE MAN** – when Christ comes, no one will know where he is from – When Christ comes, will he do more miracles than this man – <u>whoever believes in me will have streams of living water within him</u> – others said he is the Christ – why didn't you bring him in – no one ever spoke the way this man does

9. woman caught in adultery – cast first stone – you have no idea where I come from and where I am going I testify for myself my other witness is the Father who sent me – Where I go you cannot go – I come from above you are from below – I always do what pleases him – the truth will set you free – everyone who sins is a slave to sin – you belong to your father the devil – can anyone prove me guilty of sin – My father whom you claim as your God glorifies me – before Abraham is born I am; at this, they tried to stone him

10. Jesus heals a man born blind – **THIS HAPPENED SO THE WORK OF GOD MIGHT BE DISPLAYED** – they brought the Pharisees the man – the man said that he is a prophet – the Jews had decided that anyone that acknowledged that Jesus was the Christ would be put out of the synagogue – **NOBODY HAS EVER HEARD OF OPENING THE EYES OF A MAN BORN BLIND; IF THIS MAN WERE NOT FROM GOD HE COULD DO NOTHING** – How dare you lecture us, and they threw him out – Jesus found him later, and he believed Jesus was the Christ

11. The shepherd and the sheep – I have come that they may have life and have it to the full – the good Shepard lays down his life for the sheep – <u>If you are the Christ, tell us plainly</u> – **I DID TELL YOU, BUT YOU DO NOT BELIEVE** – the miracles I do in my Father's name speak for me – the sheep listen to my voice; I know them, and they follow me – again the Jews picked up stones to stone him because you claim to be God – quotes psalms 82 – I am God's son believe the miracles

12. Lazarus – the sickness will not end in death. No, it is for God's glory so that God's son will be glorified – he was deeply moved and wept – many put their faith in him, but some went to the Pharisees – **IF WE LET HIM KEEP ON LIKE THIS, EVERYONE WILL BELIEVE IN HIM, AND THE ROMANS WILL COME AND TAKE AWAY BOTH OUR PLACE AND OUR NATION** – the high priest said it is better that one die for the people than a whole nation perish <u>– the high priest that year prophesied that Jesus would die for the Jewish nation to bring them together and make them one –</u> so from that day they plotted to kill Jesus

13. Mary anoints Jesus with a pint of pure nard – a large crowd came to see Jesus and Lazarus – triumphal entry – Look how the whole world has gone after him – unless a kernel of wheat falls to the ground and dies, it remains only a single seed – Father save me from this hour – the voice from heaven came for the benefit of those there – we have heard from the Law that the Christ will remain forever – Quote from OT – **ISAIAH SAID THIS BECAUSE HE SAW JESUS' GLORY AND SPOKE ABOUT HIM** – I will judge the righteous, and there is a judge for the one who rejects me

14. **HE SHOWED THEM the FULL EXTENT OF HIS LOVE** – Now that I have washed your feet, you also should wash one another's feet – you will be blessed if you do them – Jesus predicts

his betrayal – I am telling you now before it happens so that when it happens, you will believe – tells Judas to go; **SOME THOUGHT THEY WERE TELLING HIM TO BUY WHAT WAS NEEDED OF TO GIVE SOMETHING TO THE POOR** – a new command I give you: love one another as I have loved you so you must love one another – by this men will know you are my disciples

15. Do not let your hearts be troubled – **TRUST IN GOD TRUST ALSO IN ME – I AM THE WAY AND THE TRUTH AND THE LIFE. NO ONE COMES TO THE FATHER EXCEPT THROUGH ME** – You do know him and have seen him – anyone who has seen me has also seen the Father – **AT LEAST BELIEVE ON THE EVIDENCE OF THE MIRACLES THEMSELVES** – I will do whatever you ask in my name so that the Son may bring glory to the Father – **IF YOU LOVE ME YOU WILL OBEY WHAT I COMMAND – THE WORLD WILL NO LONGER SEE ME ANYMORE, BUT YOU WILL SEE ME – BECAUSE I LIVE, YOU WILL ALSO LIVE – I AM IN THE FATHER, AND YOU ARE IN ME, AND I AM IN YOU** – If anyone loves me, he will obey my teaching – **THE COUNSELOR THE HOLY SPIRIT WILL TEACH AND REMIND YOU OF EVERYTHING** – the father is greater than I – the prince of this world is coming – **HE HAS NO HOLD ON ME BUT THE WORLD MUST LEARN THAT I LOVE THE FATHER AND DO EXACTLY WHAT HE COMMANDS**

16. vine and branches – **NO BRANCH CAN BEAR FRUIT BY ITSELF IT MUST REMAIN IN THE VINE – IF A MAN REMAINS IN ME HE WILL BEAR MUCH FRUIT – IF YOU REMAIN IN ME I WILL GIVE YOU WHATEVER YOU ASK** – if you obey you will remain in my love – **MY COMMAND IS THIS LOVE EACH OTHER AS I HAVE LOVED YOU** – You are my friends if you do what I command – If the world hates you remember it hated me first – If I had not come and spoken to them then they would not be guilty of sin – they have seen these miracles yet they hated both me and my father –

17. All this I have told you so that you will not go astray – **A TIME IS COMING WHEN ANYONE WHO KILLS YOU WILL THINK HE IS OFFERING A SERVICE TO GOD** – the prince of this world now stands condemned – you will weep while the world rejoices, but your grief will turn to joy – **MY FATHER WILL GIVE YOU WHATEVER YOU ASK IN MY NAME – I WILL**

NOT ASK THE FATHER ON YOUR BEHALF; NO THE FATHER HIMSELF LOVES YOU BECAUSE YOU LOVE ME AND HAVE BELIEVED I HAVE COME FROM GOD – You believe at Last! – **IN THE WORLD, YOU WILL HAVE TROUBLE**

18. Jesus prays for himself, his disciples, and all believers – **GLORY HAS COME TO ME THROUGH THEM** – my prayer is that you do not take them out of the world but that you protect them from the evil one – they are not of this world even as I am not of this world –

19. Jesus arrested – **MEN FALL DOWN WHEN HE SAYS HE IS JESUS** – goes to High priest – I spoke the truth why did you strike me – Peter denies Christ – before Pilate –

20. Jesus was sentenced by Pilate – because he claimed to be the son of God -the crucifixion and death – not one of his bones broken and body pierced – 2 men took Jesus's body and laid him in a tomb

21. Empty tomb – appears to women **THEY STILL DIDN'T UNDERSTAND THAT JESUS HAD TO RISE FROM THE DEAD** – appears to disciples – appears to Thomas – unless I see the nail marks… -

22. Jesus appears to the disciples while they are fishing – **TELLS them TO THROW the NET OVER AGAIN, AND THEY CATCH A 153 LARGE FISH** – Jesus reinstates Peter – books not large enough to contain everything Jesus ever did

Acts

1. Jesus was taken to heaven – Matthias has chosen to replace Judas

2. Holy Spirit comes and rests on the 120 like tongues of fire – spoke in tongues to crowd repent and be baptized in the name of Jesus Christ for the forgiveness of your sins, and you will receive the gift of the Holy Spirit – fellowship of believers

3. Peter heals a man crippled from birth – then speaks to the onlookers – **BY FAITH IN THE NAME OF JESUS THIS MAN WAS MADE STRONG – REPENT AND TURN TO GOD THAT YOUR SINS MAY BE WIPED OUT THAT TIMES OF REFRESHING MAY COME FROM THE LORD**

4. Peter and John before the Sanhedrin – seized them and put them in Jail – Salvation is found in no one else for there is no other name under heaven given to men by which we must be saved – **EVERY ONE KNEW THEY HAD DONE AN OUTSTANDING MIRACLE** – the cripple was over 40 years old – released and meet and prayed and filled with the holy spirit the place was shaken – believers share everything

5. Ananias and Sapphira lie to the holy spirit – **APOSTLES HEAL MANY** – apostles arrested by the Sadducees released by an angel to tell the full message of this new life – brought to the Sanhedrin and then released and flogged

6. choosing of the seven – not right to neglect the ministry to wait on tables – Stephan seized – face like an angel

7. Stephan's speech and stoning

8. the church persecuted and scattered – Phillip goes to Samaria – **SIMON THE SORCERER** – when they arrived, they prayed for them because they did not have the Holy Spirit, although they were baptized – Philip and the Ethiopian

9. **SAUL'S CONVERSION** – he got up and was baptized – Saul in Damascus and Jerusalem – Peter heals a paralytic and Dorcas from death

10. Cornelius calls for Peter – Peter's vision – Peter at Cornelius' house- they receive the spirit and speak in tongues, then they are baptized

11. Peter explains his actions – the Holy Spirit came on them as it did us at the beginning – you will baptize with the holy spirit – who was I to oppose God – **GOD HAS GRANTED EVEN THE GENTILES REPENTANCE UNTO LIFE** – Antioch – Greeks also learned the good news – **FIRST CALLED CHRISTIANS AT ANTIOCH**

12. **HEROD ARREST SOME, INCLUDING JAMES, AND HAD HIM PUT TO DEATH WITH THE SWORD** – Peter arrested – church earnestly prayed to God for him – Angel releases Peter – **GUARDS EXECUTED** – Herod dies

13. Barnabas and Saul **SENT OFF WITH FASTING AND PRAYER** – proconsul converted – Paul's speech – **EVERYONE ONE WHO BELIEVES IS JUSTIFIED FROM EVERYTHING YOU COULD NOT BE JUSTIFIED BY THE LAW OF MOSES** – goes to Gentiles

14. In Lystra and Derbe – he healed a man crippled from birth – called Gods, and people came to offer sacrifices to them – he told them to turn from worthless things in the past; he let all nations go their own way – Jews from Antioch stirred up the crowd and **STONED HIM AND LEFT HIM FOR DEAD** – return to Syria and appoint elders with prayer and fasting –

15. Council at Jerusalem agreed that circumcision was not required sends a letter to Gentile believers – Paul and Barnabas had a sharp disagreement and separate

16. Timothy joins Paul and Silas – he is circumcised first – goes to Macedonia – converts Lydia – heals slave girl – thrown in prison – earthquake – **CONVERT JAILER AND FAMILY** – tells the magistrates they are Romans and are apologized to

17. In Thessalonica – **JEWS WERE JEALOUS AND ROUNDED UP. SOME BAD CHARACTERS FORMED A MOB AND STARTED A RIOT** – In Berea – more character because they examined the scriptures to see if what Paul taught was true – In Athens – Unknown God – God did tthis so men would seek him and find him although he is not far from each one of us – in the past, God overlooked such ignorance but now commands everyone to repent

18. In Corinth – Paul stayed with tentmakers and worked, but when Silas and Timothy came devoted himself to preaching – **SYNAGOGUE RULER WAS CONVERTED** – Jews united to bring Paul to jail – magistrate refused to listen to them and RELEASED PAUL – THE

JEWS TURNED ON **SOSTHENES THE SYNAGOGUE RULER AND BEAT HIM ON THE COURT STEPS** – to Syria – Paul cuts hair off for a vow – **PRISCILLA AND AQUILA TAKE APOLLOS ASIDE AND TEACH HIM THE WAY MORE ADEQUATELY APOLLOS BAPTIZED BY JOHN THEN** converted to Jesus refutes the Jews in public debate –

19. In Ephesus – told to be baptized in Jesus's name to receive the Holy Spirit – God did extraordinary miracles through Paul so that even handkerchiefs and aprons healed the sick – Some Jews went around trying to drive out demons by saying In the name of Jesus whom Paul preaches I command you to come out – **I KNOW JESUS AND PAUL BUT WHO ARE YOU – THEN THE MAN BEAT THE JEWS** – riot in Ephesus – makers of idols stir up a city

20. Paul left various places because the Jews plotted against him - felt the holy spirit was leading him to Jerusalem - **RAISES MAN FROM THE DEAD FELL ASLEEP LISTENING TO PAUL** - farewell to Ephesians - Paul beaten and arrested

21. On to Jerusalem – **Paul takes a Jewish vow** – Paul arrested – When the rioters saw the soldiers, they stopped beating Paul

22. Paul speaks to the crowd - Paul declares he is a Roman citizen

23. before the Sanhedrin - Pharisees against seduces - plot to kill Paul - Paul transferred to Claudius in Caesarea

24. Trial before Felix - high priest came to Caesarea to accuse Paul - **NAZARENE SECT - THE WAY - RESURRECTION OF ALL -** when I find it more convenient - 2 years in prison there

25. Trial before Festus - appeals to Caeser - before King Agrippa

26. cont. - why should anyone considers it incredible that God raises the dead - **PROVE REPENTANCE BY DEEDS** - you are out of your mind - your great learning is driving you insane - **DO YOU THINK IN A SHORT TIME YOU CAN PERSUADE ME TO BE A CHRISTIAN**

27. **PAUL SAILS TO ROME** - storm - hurricane - shipwreck - all 276 safe

28. Ashore on Malta - **snake bite** - heals many on the island -arrives at Rome to many brothers - preaches to Jews and Gentiles

Romans

1. "That you and I may be mutually encouraged by each other's faith" – **"THE RIGHTEOUS WILL LIVE BY FAITH"** – God's wrath against mankind – "gave them over to shameful lusts. Even their women… In the same way men…in themselves the due penalty for their perversion." – "They have become filled with every kind of wickedness… they invent ways of doing evil."

2. "God's judgment against those who do such things is based on truth." – **"GOD'S KINDNESS LEADS YOU TOWARD REPENTANCE"** – To those who, by persistence in doing good, seek glory, honor, and immortality, he will give eternal life. Those who are self-seeking and who reject the truth and follow evil …" – **"NOT THOSE WHO HEAR THE LAW… BUT IT IS THOSE WHO OBEY" THAT ARE RIGHTEOUS** – "when Gentiles, who do not have the law…" – "God's name is blasphemed among the Gentiles because of you (bad Jews)" – No a man is a Jew if he is one inwardly … circumcision of the heart by the spirit not by the written code."

3. **WHAT ADVANTAGE TO BEING A JEW; FIRST OF ALL, THEY HAVE BEEN ENTRUSTED WITH THE VERY WORDS OF GOD** – Jews and Gentiles alike are all under sin – No one will be declared righteous in his sight by observing the law; rather through the law we become conscious of sin – **BUT NOW A RIGHTEOUSNESS APART FROM LAW HAS BEEN MADE KNOWN** – this righteousness from God comes through faith in Jesus Christ to all who believe – are justified freely by his grace - **WE MAINTAIN THAT A MAN IS JUSTIFIED BY FAITH APART FROM OBSERVING THE LAW**

4. Abraham believed God, and it was credited to him as righteousness – blessed is the man whom God credits righteousness apart from works – Abraham was righteous before he was circumcised – It was not through the law that he was righteous – the promise comes by faith – He is the father of us all – **BEING FULLY PERSUADED THAT GOD HAD the POWER TO DO WHAT HE PROMISED THIS IS WHY IT IS CREDITED TO HIM AS RIGHTEOUSNESS** – not to him alone but to us also who believe in him who was raised from the dead

5. since we have been justified through faith, we have peace – **REJOICE IN SUFFERINGS BRING PERSEVERANCE BRING CHARACTER, BRING HOPE, AND HOPE DOES NOT DISAPPOINT US BECAUSE GOD HAS POURED OUT HIS LOVE INTO OUR HEARTS BY THE HOLY SPIRIT –** while we were still sinners Christ died for us – **WHEN WE WERE GOD'S ENEMIES WE WERE RECONCILED HOW MUCH MORE HAVING BEEN RECONCILED SHALL WE BE SAVED THROUGH HIS LIFE** – Just as sin entered the world through one man – the gift is not like the trespass by the grace of one man overflow to the many – the gift followed many trespasses and brought justification – one trespass brings condemnation to all (ADAM) one act of righteousness brings life to all (CHRIST) –

6. We died to sin – <u>all of us who were baptized into Christ were baptized into his death</u> – anyone who has died has been freed from sin – he (Christ) cannot die again – count yourselves dead to sin but alive to God in Christ – do not let sin reign in your mortal body – **sin shall not be your master because you are not under law but under grace** - - you have been set free of sin and have become slaves to righteousness – leading to holiness – slave to sin you were free from the control of righteousness

7. her husband dies she is released from that law and is not an adulteress even if she remarries – **NOW BY DYING TO WHAT ONCE BOUND US WE HAVE BEEN RELEASED FROM THE LAW SO THAT WE SERVE IN THE NEW WAY OF THE SPIRIT AND NOT IN THE OLD WAY OF THE WRITTEN CODE** – <u>I would not know what sin was except for the law</u> – <u>sin seizing the opportunity afforded by the commandment produced in me every kind of covetous desire</u> – I found that the very commandment that was intended to bring life actually brought death – sin deceived me – **I DO NOT UNDERSTAND WHAT I DO. FOR WHAT I WANT TO DO I DO NOT DO, BUT WHAT I HATE TO DO** – <u>it is not me that does it but sin living in me</u> – I see another law at work in my body waging war against the law of my mind and making me a prisoner to the law of sin – **WHAT A WRETCHED MAN I AM** – in my mind am a slave to God's law – but in the sinful nature a slave to the law of sin

8. there is no condemnation for those who are in Jesus – the law of the Spirit of life set me free from the law of sin – for what the law was powerless to do in that it was weakened by the sinful nature God did

by sending his own Son as a sin offering – in order that the righteous requirements of the law might be meet in us – you are controlled by the spirit if the spirit of god lives in you – if Christ is in you, you are dead to sin – those who are led by the spirit are sons of god – the Spirit himself testifies with our spirit – **THE CREATION WAITS IN EAGER EXPECTATION FOR THE SONS OF GOD TO BE REVEALED** – hope that is seen is not hope at all – in the same way the Spirit helps us in our weakness – helps us pray – in all things God works for the good of those who love him – if God is for us who can be against us – Jesus is at the right hand of God and is interceding for us – nothing can separate us from the love of God –

9. Paul wishes to be cut off from Christ for the sake of his brothers of his own race – They were adopted, divine glory, the covenants, the receiving of the law, the temple worship, the patriarchs, and the promises and the ancestry of Jesus – **IT IS NOT THE NATURAL CHILDREN WHO ARE GOD'S CHILDREN BUT THE CHILDREN OF THE PROMISE WHO ARE REGARDED AS ABRAHAM'S OFFSPRING** – God has mercy on whom he wants to have mercy, and he hardens whom he wants to harden – Does the potter have the right to make out of the same lump of clay some for noble purposes and some for common use – what if he did this to make the riches of his glory known to the objects of his mercy – **THE GENTILES HAVE OBTAINED RIGHTEOUSNESS BY FAITH, BUT ISRAEL PURSUED A LAW OF RIGHTEOUSNESS HAS NOT OBTAINED IT – BECAUSE THEY PURSUED IT NOT BY FAITH BUT AS IF IT WERE WORKS –**

10. "Christ is the end of the law so that there may be righteousness for everyone who believes" – the word is near you; it is in your mouth and in your heart – confess that Jesus is Lord and believe God raised him from the dead you are saved – the Lord is Lord of all –

11. Did God reject his people – so too, at this present time, there is a remnant chosen by grace, and if by grace, then it is no longer by works – what Israel sought so earnestly it did not obtain, but the elect did – because of their transgression salvation has come to the Gentiles to make Israel envious – I am the apostle to the gentiles – gentiles to be grafted in and God can graft the fallen branches of the Jews – Israel has experienced a hardening in part until the full number of the Gentiles has come in – you have received mercy as a result of their disobedience

12. <u>Offer your bodies as living sacrifices – this is your spiritual act of worship</u> – **BE TRANSFORMED BY THE RENEWING OF YOUR MIND, THEN YOU WILL BE ABLE TO TEST AND APPROVE WHAT GOD'S WILL IS** – hate what is evil cling to what is good – List of good traits – Love is – live at peace with everyone if it is possible – Do not be overcome by evil but overcome evil with good

13. Submit to authorities – they exist because of God – this is why you pay taxes, revenue, respect, and honor – Love does not harm its neighbor – love is the fulfillment of the Law – clothe yourselves with the Lord Jesus Christ and do not think how to gratify the desires of the sinful nature

14. Accept him whose faith is weak and do not pass judgment – **ONE MAN'S FAITH ALLOWS HIM TO EAT ANYTHING. ANOTHER DOES NOT ONE CONSIDERS ONE DAY TO BE SPECIAL ANOTHER NOT** – do not judge but worry about how to give your account to God – the kingdom of god is not a matter of eating and drinking but of righteousness, peace, and joy in the Holy spirit – make every effort to do what leads to peace – all food is clean, but it is wrong to eat anything that causes someone else to sin – <u>whatever you believe about these things keep between you and god</u> – a man who has doubts but eats is condemned

15. We who are strong ought to bear the failings of the weak – <u>everything that was written in the past was written to teach us</u> – accept one another then just as Christ accepted you – Christ became a servant to the Jews to confirm the promises – It has always been my ambition to preach the gospel where Christ was not known … - <u>but now there is no more place for me to work in these regions</u> – I am on my way to Jerusalem – **PRAY TO GOD FOR ME** –

16. personal greetings – commends many, including many women – All the churches of Christ send greeting

I Corinthians

1. Some say I follow Paul, another Apollos, etc. – Was Paul crucified
    for you? – came to preach, not baptize; **NOT WITH WORDS OF
    HUMAN WISDOM LEST THE CROSS OF CHRIST BE
    EMPTIED OF ITS POWER** – the message of the cross is
    foolishness to those who are perishing – **WE PREACH CHRIST
    CRUCIFIED A STUMBLING BLOCK TO JEWS AND
    FOOLISHNESS TO THE GENTILES** – God chooses the foolish
    things of this world to shame the wise – so that no one may boast
    before him –

2. We speak of God's secret wisdom, a wisdom that has been hidden,
    and God destined for glory before time – God has revealed it to us by
    his spirit – The spirit searches all things, even the deep things of God
    – what we speak… are taught by the spirit expressing spiritual truths
    in spiritual words – **SPIRITUAL MAN IS NOT SUBJECT TO
    ANY MAN'S JUDGMENT** – we have the mind of Christ

3. divisions of the church – **YOU ARE WORLDLY IF YOU CLAIM
    TO BE OF MEN** – each one will be shown for what they build –
    **"DON'T YOU KNOW THAT YOU YOURSELVES ARE
    GOD'S TEMPLE AND THAT GOD'S SPIRIT LIVES IN
    YOU?'** God's temple is sacred and you are that temple - you
    should become a fool to learn the truth – you are of Christ and Christ
    is of God

4. men ought to regard us as servants of Christ and as those entrusted
    with the secret things of God – I do not even judge myself – Do not
    go beyond what is written – His very hour we go hungry and thirsty
    we are in rags we are brutally raised we work hard with our own
    hands – **WHEN WE ARE CURSED WE BLESS; PERSECUTED
    WE ENDURE IT; SLANDER WE ANSWER KINDLY; UP TO
    THIS MOMENT WE HAVE BECOME THE SCUM OF THE
    EARTH** – I became your father through the gospel – he (Timothy)
    will remind you of my way of life in Christ Jesus

5. it is reported that there is sexual immorality among you – **HAND
    THIS MAN OVER TO SATAN SO THAT THE SINFUL
    NATURE MAY BE DESTROYED AND HIS SPIRIT SAVED** –
    I wrote not to associate with sexually immoral people; not meaning

of the world but in the church – expel the wicked man from among you

6. if you have disputes appoint even men of little account in the church as judges – **THE VERY FACT THAT YOU HAVE LAWSUITS AMONG YOU MEANS THAT YOU HAVE BEEN COMPLETELY DEFEATED ALREADY** – Why not rather be wronged and cheated? – food for the stomach and stomach for food. **THE BODY IS NOT MEANT FOR SEXUAL IMMORALITY** – your bodies are members of Christ himself – **UNITE WITH A PROSTITUTE AND BECOME ONE WITH HER** – all sins a man commits are outside his body except sexual sins – your body is a temple – you are not your own you were bought with a price – honor God with your body

7. Marriage – husband's and wife's bodies belong to each other too – I wish everyone to remain unmarried – those who marry will face many troubles in this life – an unmarried man or woman is concerned about the Lord's affairs –

8. food and idols - **KNOWLEDGE PUFFS UP BUT LOVE BUILDS UP** - Food does not bring us near to god - EATING IN AN IDOLS TEMPLE - weak brother destroyed by your knowledge

9. Rights of an apostle - right to take a believing wife - those who work in the temple get their food from the temple - to the Jew, I became a Jew - weak became weak, not under the law, etc.

10. **THEY WERE ALL BAPTIZED INTO MOSES IN THE CLOUD AND IN THE SEA – NEVER LESS GOD WAS NOT PLEASED WITH MOST OF THEM, AND THEIR BODIES WERE SCATTERED OVER THE DESERT** – If you think you are standing firm beware that you do not fall – no temptation except what is common to man – **HE WILL NOT LET YOU BE TEMPTED BEYOND WHAT YOU CAN BEAR** – when you are tempted he will provide a way out – scarifies of pagans are offered to demons – and I do not want you to be participants with demons – **NOBODY SHOULD SEEK HIS OWN GOOD BUT THE GOOD OF OTHERS** – if an unbeliever asks you overeat whatever is put in front of you but if he says this has been offered in sacrifice do not eat it for your conscience and his – whether you eat or drink do all for the glory of God – I am not seeking my good but the good of the many so that they may be saved –

11. head of every man is Christ and head of the woman is a man, and the head of Christ is God – **A MAN SHOULD HAVE SHORT HAIR AND A WOMAN LONG** – man and woman are not independent of each other – your meetings do more harm than good – **THERE HAVE TO BE DIFFERENCES AMONG YOU TO SHOW WHICH OF YOU HAVE GOD'S APPROVAL** – whenever you eat the cup or the bread you proclaim the Lord's death until he comes – eats in a manner that is unworthy is sinning – when we are judged by the world we are being disciplined so that we will not be condemned

12. I do not want you to be ignorant; you know, when you were pagans, somehow or other, you influenced and led astray to mute idols – **THERE ARE DIFFERENT KINDS OF SERVICE BUT THE SAME LORD** – different kinds of working but the same god – gifts; wisdom, knowledge, faith, healing, miraculous powers, prophecy, tongues, distinguishing spirits, interpretation of tongues – All are the works of one spirit – we are all given the one Spirit to drink – the body is made of many parts – Eye cannot say to the hand I do not need you – you are the body of Christ

13. **LOVE** – faith but have not love I am nothing – **LOVE ALWAYS PROTECTS, TRUSTS, HOPES, PERSEVERES** – I know in part – 3 things remain faith, hope, and love

14. Gifts addressed – **I PRAY WITH MY SPIRIT AND MIND SING WITH SPIRIT AND MIND** – tongues are a sign for unbelievers, not believers – orderly worship – the spirits of a prophet are under the control of the prophet – **DISGRACEFUL FOR A WOMAN TO SPEAK IN WORSHIP SAID 2 TIMES –**

15. Christ appeared to Paul last – Paul worked harder than all of them – if Christ is raised from the dead, how can you preach there is no resurrection – **ADAM BROUGHT DEATH CHRIST BROUGHT RESURRECTION THE LAST ENEMY UNDER HIS FEET IS DEATH** – why are people baptized for the dead – resurrection body – **our earthly body is like a seed it will be planted and out of it will come our spiritual body** – the sting of death is sin

16. collection of god's people – the first day of the week like the Galatians – be on guard, stand firm, be men of courage, be strong, do everything in love –

II Corinthians

1. God comforts us in all our troubles so that we can comfort others – we were under great pressure beyond our ability to endure – but it happened so that we might rely on God and not on ourselves – you help us with your prayers – God anointed us set his seal on us and put his spirit in us as a deposit

2. <u>you ought to forgive and comfort the sinner so that he will not be overwhelmed by excessive sorrow</u> – in order that Satan might not outwit us – **WE HAVE THE AROMA OF CHRIST**

3. a new covenant not of the letter but the spirit for the letter kills, and the spirit saves – **IF THE MINISTRY THAT CONDEMNS MEN IS GLORIOUS, THEN HOW MUCH MORE GLORIOUS THE MINISTRY THAT BRINGS RIGHTEOUSNESS** – since we have such a hope, we are very bold – to this day the veil remains when the old covenant is read – **REFLECT THE LORD'S GLORY**

4. we have renounced shameful and secret ways – if our gospel is veiled, it is veiled to the perishing – the god of this age has blinded the minds of the unbelievers – we have this treasure in jars of clay – we always carry around in our body the death of Christ – outwardly we are wasting away yet inwardly we are being renewed day by day – momentary troubles are achieving for us eternal glory – what is seen is temporary but what is unseen is eternal

5. we have an earthly tent; when it is destroyed, we will have an eternal house in heaven – the spirit is a deposit – we live by faith, not by sight – you can answer those who take pride in what is seen rather than what is in the heart – **ONE DIED FOR ALL THEREFORE ALL DIED** – we should no longer live for ourselves, but the one who died for us – in Christ is a new creation – God reconciled us through Christ and gave us the ministry of reconciliation – God reconciled the world to himself in Christ not counting men's sins against them – we are giving the message of reconciliation We are Christ's ambassadors – God made him who had no sin to be sin so that we might become the righteousness of God

6. we urge you not to receive God's grace in vain – Paul's hardships, including hard work and sleepless nights – we are not withholding our affection from you by you are withholding from us – **WHAT**

AGREEMENT IS THERE BETWEEN THE TEMPLE OF GOD AND IDOLS? WE ARE THE TEMPLE OF THE LIVING GOD; DO NOT BE YOKED WITH UNBELIEVERS – come out and be separate from them

7. since we have these promises, let us purify ourselves from everything that contaminates the body and spirit – in all our troubles, my joy knows no bounds – your concern for me so that my joy was greater than ever – I see my letter hurt you but only for a while; your sorrow led to repentance – **SORROW LEADS TO REPENTANCE THAT LEADS TO SALVATION AND LEAVES NO REGRET BUT WORLDLY SORROW LEADS TO DEATH** –

8. in their extreme poverty welled up in rich generosity gave beyond their ability – gave themselves first to the Lord and then to us – see that you excel in the grace of giving – Last year you were the first to give and the first to have the desire to do so – our desire is that no others might be relieved while you are hard pressed but that there might be equality – Titus sent to Corinth

9. Finish the arrangements for the generous gift you promised. Then it will be ready as a generous gift, not as one given grudgingly given – each should give what he has decided in his heart … **GOD LOVES A CHEERFUL GIVER – GOD IS ABLE TO MAKE ALL GRACE ABOUND TO YOU SO THAT IN ALL THINGS AND ALL TIMES YOU HAVE ALL YOU NEED** – he who supplies the seed will also supply the increase so that you can **BE GENEROUS ON ALL OCCASIONS AND RESULT IN THANKSGIVING** – is also overflowing in many expressions of thanks to God – in their prayers their hearts will go out to you –

10. Paul timid when face to face but bold when away – **WE WAGE WAR WITH WEAPONS OF DIVINE POWER TO DEMOLISH STRONGHOLDS** – I do not want to seem to be trying to frighten you with my letters – Our hope is that as you grow in faith, we can go out to the outlying areas and preach the gospel –

11. I do not think I am inferior to the super-apostles – I preached free of charge but robbed other churches to preach to you – false apostles, deceitful no wonder Satan masquerades as an angel of light himself – **YOU PUT UP WITH ANYONE WHO ENSLAVES YOU OR EXPLOITS YOU OR TAKES ADVANTAGE OF YOU OR PUSHES HIMSELF FORWARD OR SLAPS YOU IN THE**

FACE – 5 times received 40 lashes – 3 times beaten – stoned 1 time – 3 times shipwrecked – besides everything I face daily the pressure of my concern for all the churches

12. **I KNOW A MAN WHO 14 YEARS AGO WAS CAUGHT UP IN THE 3ᴿᴰ HEAVEN** – to keep me from becoming conceited, I was given a thorn in the flesh – things that mark an apostle sign, wonders, and miracles – **I DON'T WANT YOUR POSSESSIONS I WANT YOU** – I fear you will be quarreling, an outburst of anger, and have not repented of your impurity, sexual sins…

13. **EXAMINE YOURSELVES TO SEE WHETHER YOU ARE IN FAITH. TEST YOURSELVES. - DON'T YOU REALIZE THAT JESUS IS IN YOU UNLESS OF COURSE YOU FAIL THE TEST** – I write to you so that when I come, these things will be taken care of – aim for perfection

Galatians

1. even if an angel from heaven or we preach a gospel other than the one we preached to you, let him be eternally condemned – Paul converted and went to Arabia, then Damascus, then 3 years later to Jerusalem to meet with Peter and James for 15 days

2. 14 years later went up to Jerusalem again and met with the leaders – he wanted to make sure he was preaching correctly – they added nothing to his message – He to the Gentiles, Peter to the Jews – asked to continue to remember the poor – Paul opposes peter about circumcision – even Barnabas had been led astray – **IF RIGHTEOUSNESS COULD BE GAINED THROUGH THE LAW, THEN CHRIST DIED FOR NOTHING!**

3. <u>Did you receive the Spirit by observing the law</u> – after beginning with the Spirit are you trying to attain your goal through human effort – those who believe are children of Abraham – <u>those who rely on the law are under a curse</u> – **CHRIST REDEEMED US FROM THE CURSE OF THE LAW BY BECOMING A CURSE FOR US** – The law introduced 430 years after the promise to Abraham does not set aside the covenant and do away with the promise – **PURPOSE OF THE LAW – WAS ADDED BECAUSE OF THE TRANSGRESSIONS UNTIL THE SEED TO WHOM THE PROMISE REFERRED HAD COME** – if a law had been given that could impart life then righteousness would have come from the law – before faith came we were held prisoners by the law locked up until faith could be revealed **THE LAW WAS PUT IN CHARGE TO LEAD US TO CHRIST THAT WE MIGHT BE JUSTIFIED BY FAITH** – <u>Now that faith has come we are no longer under the supervision of the law</u> – all baptized into Christ have clothed yourself with Christ

4. <u>when we were children, we were in slavery until the son came to redeem those under the law that we might have full rights of sons</u> – Because you are sons, God sent the spirit of his son into our hearts – now you know god or rather are known by God – It is fine to be zealous as long as the purpose is good – until Christ is formed in you – Hagar and Sarah – one represents slaves and the other freedom –

5. it is for freedom that Christ has set us free – do not let yourselves be burdened by the yoke of slavery – **IF CIRCUMCISED HE IS OBLIGATED TO OBEY THE WHOLE LAW** – you are trying to be justified by the law have fallen away from grace – **THE ONLY THING THAT COUNTS IS FAITH EXPRESSING ITSELF THROUGH LOVE** – you are called to be free do not use your freedom to indulge the sinful nature – the entire law is summed up in a single command Love your neighbor as yourself – live by the spirit, and you will not gratify the sinful nature – **IF YOU ARE LED BY THE SPIRIT YOU ARE NOT UNDER THE LAW** – Acts of sinful nature – the fruit of the spirit

6. Carry each other's burdens – each should carry his own load – anyone who receives instruction in the word must share all good things with the instructor – **LET US NOT BECOME WEARY IN DOING GOOD** – let us do good to all people, especially to those who belong in the family – people are circumcised to avoid persecution for the cross of Christ – what counts is a new creation

Ephesians

1. he chose us in him before the creation of the world – he predestined us – he made know to us the mystery of his will according to his good pleasure – we were chosen having been predestined – **HIM WHO WORKS OUT EVERYTHING IN CONFORMITY WITH HIS PURPOSE** – having believed you were marked in him with a seal – I keep asking the father to give you wisdom so that you may know him better – I pray that the eyes of your heart may be enlightened – **THAT YOU MAY KNOW THE HOPE... THE RICHES... GREAT POWER THAT HE EXERTED WHEN HE RAISED CHRIST FROM THE DEAD** – god placed everything under his feet –

2. you were dead in your transgressions and sins – when you followed the ways of the world and of the ruler of the kingdom of the air – **ALL OF US ALSO LIVED AMONG THEM AT ONE TIME** – God who is rich in mercy made us alive with Christ even when we were dead in transgression – **IT IS BY GRACE THAT YOU ARE SAVED, THROUGH FAITH** – it is a gift of god not works – we are created to do good works – once far away have been brought near – **ABOLISHING IN HIS FLESH THE LAW WITH ITS COMMANDMENTS AND REGULATIONS** – to reconcile both of them to God through the cross – built on the foundations of the apostles and prophets with Jesus the chief cornerstone

3. you will be able to understand my insight into the mystery of Christ, which was not made known to men in other generations, as it has been revealed by the spirit to God's holy apostles and prophets – In him and through Him, we may approach God with freedom and confidence – to have the power to grasp how wide... deep... long... high is the love of Christ and to know that this love surpasses knowledge – **TO HIM WHO IS ABLE TO DO MORE THAN WE ASK....**

4. I urge you to live a life worthy of the calling – one lord, one faith, one baptism... God... Father – But to each of us grace has been given as Christ apportioned it – He gave some to be apostles some to be prophets.... – to prepare God's people for works of service so that the body will be built up – **darkened in understanding... separated from god... hardening of their hearts ... lost all**

sensitivity…. **Given themselves over to sensuality so as to indulge in every kind of impurity … continual lust for more** – to be made new in the attitude of your minds and to **PUT ON YOUR NEW SELF CREATED TO BE LIKE GOD IN TRUE RIGHTEOUSNESS AND HOLINESS** – in your anger do not let the sun go down – do not give the devil a foothold – do not let any unwholesome talk come out of your mouths but only what is helpful in building – do not grieve the Holy Spirit – Get rid of all bitterness, rage…

5. Be imitators of God as dearly loved children – **LIVE A LIFE OF LOVE JUST AS CHRIST LOVED US** – there must not be even a hint of sexual immorality, impurity, greed…coarse joking…. – live as children of the light – find out what pleases the lord – **SHAMEFUL TO EVEN MENTION WHAT THE DISOBEDIENT DO IN SECRET** – make the most of every opportunity **UNDERSTAND WHAT THE LORD'S WILL IS** – be filled with the spirit speak to one another in psalms, hymns, and spiritual songs and **MAKE MUSIC IN YOUR HEART TO THE LORD ALWAYS GIVING THANKS** – submit to one another – Wives to husbands – husbands love you wife – for this reason a man will leave his father and mother and be united to his wife and the two will become one flesh this is a profound mystery – wife must respect her husband

6. Children obey your parents in the lord – **FATHERS DO NOT EXASPERATE YOUR CHILDREN, BRING THEM UP IN THE TRAINING AND INSTRUCTION OF THE LORD** – slaves obey your master – serve wholeheartedly as if serving the lord – master treat your slaves in the same way – **PUT ON THE FULL ARMOR OF GOD** – take a stand against the devil's schemes – our struggle is not against flesh and blood but against… the dark world … the spiritual forces of evil in the heavenly realms – the belt of truth – the breastplate of righteousness – shield of peace – helmet of salvation - **SWORD OF THE SPIRIT WHICH IS THE WORD OF GOD** – pray in the spirit on all occasions with all kinds of prayers and requests – always keep on praying for all the saints – Pray also for me pray that I might declare it fearlessly

Philippians

1. This is my prayer that your love may abound more and more in knowledge and depth of insight; so that you may be able to discern what is best and may be pure and blameless – the important thing is that Christ is preached in every way whether in false motive or pure – I know that through your prayers and help given by the spirit of Jesus Christ … - **CHRIST WILL BE EXALTED IN MY BODY WHETHER BY LIFE OR DEATH** – to live is Christ to die is gain – <u>Whatever happens conduct your selves in a manner worthy of the gospel of Christ –</u> do not be frightened in any way by those who oppose you but let this be a sign that you will be saved

2. **DO NOTHING OUT OF SELFISH AMBITION OR VAIN CONCEIT BUT IN HUMILITY CONSIDER OTHERS BETTER THAN YOURSELVES** – your attitude should be the same as that of Christ **– continue to work out your salvation with fear and trembling** – do everything without complaining or arguing – the word of life –

3. rejoice in the lord – we who worship by the Spirit – Paul's qualifications for being proud – I consider everything a loss compared to the surpassing greatness of knowing Christ… - the righteousness that comes from God and is by faith – forgetting what is behind and straining toward what is ahead… - **AND IS SOME POINT YOU THINK DIFFERENTLY THAT to GOD WILL MAKE CLEAR TO YOU** – <u>their god is their stomach, and their glory is their shame their mind is on earthly things</u> …

4. Rejoice in the Lord always – **IN EVERYTHING BY PRAYER AND THANKSGIVING PRESENT YOUR REQUESTS TO GOD** – <u>finally whatever is true, whatever is noble, … think about such things –</u> **I HAVE LEARNED THE SECRET OF BEING CONTENT IN ANY AND EVERY SITUATION …** <u>I can do everything through him who gives me strength –</u> I am looking for what may be credited to your account – my god will meet your needs according to his glorious riches in Christ – **THE GRACE OF THE LORD JESUS CHRIST BE WITH YOUR SPIRIT AMEN**

Colossians

1. The word of truth, the gospel – all over the world, this gospel is bearing fruit and growing – since the day we heard about you, we have not stopped praying for you – **YOU MAY HAVE A LIFE WORTHY OF THE LORD** – Christ is the image of the invisible God – all things created through him – **HE IS THE FIRSTBORN FROM AMONG THE DEAD** – through him to reconcile to himself all things on earth or things in heaven by making peace through his blood shed on the cross – **HE HAS RECONCILED YOU BY CHRIST'S PHYSICAL BODY THROUGH DEATH TO PRESENT YOU HOLY IN HIS SIGHT** – the gospel you heard and has been proclaimed to every living creature – the mystery that has been hidden for ages has now been disclosed to the saints – **THIS MYSTERY, WHICH IS CHRIST IN YOU -**

2. **KNOW THE MYSTERY NAMELY CHRIST IN WHOM ALL THE TREASURES OF WISDOM AND KNOWLEDGE** – see to it that no one takes you captive through hollow and deceptive philosophy which depends on human tradition and the basic principles of this world – having canceled the written code and its regulations… he took it away nailing it to the cross – do not let anyone judge you by what you eat or drink – **THE LAW AND FESTIVALS WERE "BUT A SHADOW OF THE THINGS THAT WERE TO COME"** – anyone who delights in false humility and the <u>worship of angels</u> disqualify you for the prize – **SINCE YOU DIED WITH CHRIST TO THE BASIC PRINCIPLES OF THIS WORLD WHY DO YOU SUBMIT TO ITS RULES** – <u>such regulations have the appearance of wisdom … but they lack any value in restraining sensual indulgence</u>

3. **SINCE YOU HAVE BEEN RAISED WITH CHRIST, SET YOUR HEARTS ON THINGS ABOVE WHERE CHRIST IS SEATED ON THE RIGHT HAND OF GOD** – for you died and your life is now hidden with Christ in God – <u>Put to death whatever belongs to the earthly nature … you must rid yourselves of all such things … - do not lie to each other</u> – as God's chosen people … **CLOTHE YOURSELF WITH COMPASSION. OVER ALL THESE VIRTUES PUT ON LOVE WHICH BINDS THEM ALL TOGETHER IN PERFECT UNITY** – let the peace of Christ

rule in your heart – be thankful – let the word of Christ dwell in you as richly as you teach and admonish each other – with all wisdom, and as you sing psalms, hymns, and spiritual songs with gratitude in your hearts to God – Whatever you do give thanks to God the Father through him – wives submit – husbands love your wife – children, Fathers- slaves – **WHATEVER YOU DO WORK AT IT WITH ALL YOUR HEART AS MEN WORKING FOR THE LORD NOT FOR MEN**

4. devote yourselves to prayer being watchful and thankful – proclaim the mystery of Christ – make the most of every opportunity – Epaphras is always wrestling in prayer for you – Luke the doctor – after this letter is read trade letters with the Laodiceans and read their letter – remember my chains

I Thessalonians

1. **YOUR WORK PRODUCED BY FAITH** – you became imitators of us and of the Lord – you welcomed the message with joy – They tell of how you turned to God from idols to serve the living and true God

2. **WE ARE NOT TRYING TO PLEASE MEN BUT GOD WHO TESTS OUR HEARTS** – we loved you so much we not only shred the gospel but our lives as well – <u>urge you to live a life worthy of God</u> – you accepted it not as the word of men but as it actually is the word of God – we tried to come to see you, but Satan stopped us

3. Timothy's report about them

4. it is God's will that you should be sanctified, avoid sexual immorality, and learn to control your own body, in a way that is holy and honorable – **GOD DID NOT CALL US TO BE IMPURE BUT TO LIVE A HOLY LIFE**- we urge you brothers to do more and more – **MAKE IT YOUR AMBITION TO LEAD A QUIET LIFE, MIND YOUR WON BUSINESS AND TO WORK WITH YOUR HANDS** … - dead in Christ will rise first after that we who are still alive will be caught up together with them in the clouds –

5. day of the Lord will be like a thief – you are sons of the day and sons of the light – those who sleep sleep at night and those who get drunk get drunk at night – since we belong to the day, let us be self-controlled putting on faith and love as a breastplate and the hope of salvation as a helmet – respect those who work hard among you – **WARN THOSE WHO ARE IDLE ENCOURAGE THE TIMID HELP THE WEAK BE PATIENT WITH EVERYONE** – <u>be joyful always pray continually</u> – **GIVE THANKS IN ALL CIRCUMSTANCES** – test everything hold on to the good - **MAY YOUR WHOLE SPIRIT, SOUL, AND BODY BE KEPT BLAMELESS - BROTHERS PRAY FOR US**

II Thessalonians

1. we give thanks for you because your faith is growing more and more, and the love every one of you has for each other is increasing – He will pay back trouble to those who trouble you and give relief to you who are troubled – he will punish those who do not know God and do not obey the gospel – on the day he comes to be glorified in his holy people and be marveled at among those who believe – God may count you worthy of his calling and that by his power he may fulfill every good purpose of yours and every act prompted by your faith

2. for that day will come until the rebellion occurs and the man of lawlessness is revealed the man doomed to destruction – the secret poser of lawlessness is already at work – the coming of the lawless one will be in accordance with Satan displayed in all kinds of counterfeit miracles, signs, and wonders – **THEY PERISH BECAUSE THEY REFUSE TO LOVE THE TRUTH AND SO BE SAVED FOR THIS REASON GOD SENDS THEM A POWERFUL DELUSION SO THAT THEY BELIEVE A LIE** – from the beginning God chose you to be saved through the sanctifying work of the spirit – stand firm and hold to the teachings we passed on to you whether by word of mouth or letter

3. **PRAY FOR US** – <u>keep away from every brother who is idle and does not live according to the teaching</u> – **IF A MAN DOES NOT WORK, HE WILL NOT EAT – NEVER TIRE OF DOING WHAT IS RIGHT** – <u>do not associate with him yet do not regard him as an enemy but warn him as a brother</u>

I Timothy

1. command certain men not to teach false doctrines… nor devote themselves to myths and endless genealogies - **THESE PROVIDE CONTROVERSIES RATHER THAN GOD'S WORK** – <u>the goal of this command is love which comes from a pure heart and good conscience and sincere faith –</u> the law is made not for the righteous but the lawbreakers … slave traders…. – I was once a violent man – Christ came to save sinners of which I am the worst – I was shown mercy – some have rejected these and have shipwrecked their faith

2. requests, prayers, intercession, and thanksgiving be made for everyone – I want women to dress modestly – **A WOMAN SHOULD LEARN IN QUIETNESS AND FULL SUBMISSION – SHE MUST BE SILENT** – women will be saved through childbearing if they continue in faith, love, and holiness with propriety

3. Overseers and deacons – their wives are to be worthy of respect – beyond all question, the mystery of godliness is great

4. the spirit says in later times, there will be **HYPOCRITICAL LIARS. THEY WILL FORBID PEOPLE TO MARRY AND ORDER THEM TO ABSTAIN FROM CERTAIN FOODS** – God created everything is good if it is received with thanksgiving – have nothing to do with godless myths and old wives tales rather train yourself to be godly – godliness has value for all things holding promise for both the present and future life to come – don't let anyone look down on you because you are young – devote yourself to the public reading of scripture preaching and teaching – **WATCH YOUR LIFE AND DOCTRINE CLOSELY BECAUSE IF YOU DO, YOU WILL SAVE BOTH YOURSELF AND YOUR HEARERS**

5. do not rebuke an older man harshly but **EXHORT HIM AS IF HE WERE YOUR FATHER – OLDER WOMEN AS MOTHERS AND YOUNGER AS SISTERS** – <u>if anyone does not provide for his relatives, he has denied the faith and is worse than an unbeliever – no widow may be put on the list unless she is over 60 – relatives should take care of widows first –</u> **THOSE WHO SIN SHOULD BE REBUKED PUBLICLY SO THAT OTHERS MAY TAKE**

WARNING – stop drinking only water <u>use a little wine because of your stomach</u> and frequent illnesses – **THE SINS OF SOME MEN ARE OBVIOUS … IN THE SAME WAY GOOD DEED ARE OBVIOUS**

6. false teachers – he is conceited and understands nothing; he has an unhealthy interest in controversies and quarrels about words … thinks godliness is a means to financial gain – **GODLINESS WITH CONTENTMENT IS GREAT GAIN – PEOPLE WHO WANT TO GET RICH FALL INTO TEMPTATION, AND A TRAP AND INTO MANY FOOLISH AND HARMFUL DESIRES THE LOVE OF MONEY IS THE ROOT OF ALL KINDS OF EVIL** – <u>Jesus Christ while in front of Pilate made the good confession</u> – do not put your hope in wealth but in God who richly provides us with everything for our enjoyment – be rich in deeds and generous and willing to share - **TURN AWAY FROM GODLESS CHATTER AND THE OPPOSING IDEAS OF WHAT IS FALSELY CALLED KNOWLEDGE AND SOME HAVE PROFESSED AND IN SO DOING SO HAVE WANDERED FROM THE FAITH**

II Timothy

1. **GOD DID NOT GIVE US A SPIRIT OF TIMIDITY BUT A SPIRIT OF POWER OF LOVE AND SELF DISCIPLINE** – he has saved us and called us to a holy life, not because of anything we have done – yet I am not ashamed because **I KNOW WHOM I HAVE BELIEVED AND AM CONVINCED THAT HE IS ABLE TO GUARD WHAT I HAVE ENTRUSTED TO HIM FOR THAT DAY** – guard the sound teaching with the help of the Holy Spirit who lives in you

2. **NO ONE SERVING AS A SOLDIER GETS INVOLVED IN CIVILIAN AFFAIRS. HE WANTS TO PLEASE HIS COMMANDING OFFICER** – reflects on what I am saying, for the Lord will give your insight into all this – Remember Jesus Christ raised from the dead and descended from David. This is the gospel for which I am suffering – If we died with him, we also live with him if we endure… - **WARN THEM BEFORE GOD AGAINST QUARRELING ABOUT WORDS** – do your best to present yourself to God as one approved, a workman who does not need to be ashamed who correctly handles the word of truth – everyone who confesses the name of the Lord must turn away from wickedness – **SOME ARE FOR NOBLE PURPOSES SOME FOR IGNOBLE** – flee the evil desires of youth and pursue righteousness, faith and love and peace along with those who call on the Lord out of a pure heart – we must not quarrel; instead we must be kind to everyone able to teach and not resentful – those who oppose him he must gently instruct

3. **THERE WILL BE TERRIBLE TIMES IN THE LAST DAYS – LOVERS OF THEMSELVES, LOVERS OF MONEY WITHOUT LOVE, ABUSIVE UNGRATEFUL, LOVERS OF PLEASURE ETC- HAVING A FORM OF GODLINESS BUT DENYING ITS POWER** – always learning but never able to acknowledge the truth – their folly will be clear to everyone – you know about my teaching, my way of life, my purpose, faith, patience, love endurance… - everyone that wants to live a godly life in Christ will be persecuted – **ALL SCRIPTURE IS GOD-BREATHED AND IS USEFUL FOR TEACHING, REBUKING, CORRECTING AND TRAINING IN RIGHTEOUSNESS…**

4. Preach the word – **BE PREPARED IN SEASON AND OUT OF SEASON – CORRECT, REBUKE AND ENCOURAGE WITH GREAT PATIENCE AND CAREFUL INSTRUCTION** – to suit their own evil desires, they will gather around them a great number of teachers to say what their itching ears want to hear – I have fought the good fight I have finished the race… when you come , bring my cloak that I left with Carpus at Troas and my scrolls, especially the parchments – at my first defense everyone deserted me – I was delivered from the lion's mouth – I left Trophimus sick in Miletus

Titus

1. knowledge of the truth that leads to godliness, faith, and knowledge resting on the hope of eternal life – he brought his word to light – all elders must be blameless – children not wild and disobedient – pay no attention to Jewish myths – to the pure all things are pure but to those whose minds are corrupted and do notbelieve nothing is pure – they claim to know God, but by their actions they deny him

2. teach the older men – teach the older women – wives to be subject to their husbands – encourage the young men to be self-controlled – teach slaves – the grace of god that brings salvation has appeared to all men; it teaches us to say No to ungodliness and worldly passions and to live self-controlled upright and godly lives in this present life – to purify for himself a people that are his very own eager to do what is good

3. remind people to be subject to rulers – to be obedient and to do what is good – show true humility to all men – he saved us through the washing of rebirth and renewal by the Holy Spirit whom he poured out on us… through Jesus … so that having been justified by his grace, we might become heirs having the hope of eternal life – avoid foolish controversies, genealogies, arguments, quarrels about the law – warn a divisive person 1 time then again, then have nothing to do with him – he itself-condemned **– our people must learn to devote themselves to doing what is good**

Philemon

1. Archippus, our **FELLOW SOLDIER** – I pray that you may be active in sharing your faith so that you will have a full understanding of everything we have in Christ

Hebrews

1. In the past, God spoke through the prophets, but in the last days, he spoke through his Son – sustaining all things through his powerful word – he provided purification for sins – all angels are ministering spirits sent to serve those who will inherit salvation

2. we must pay careful attention so that we do not drift away – by the grace of God that he might taste death for everyone – made the author of salvation perfect through suffering – both the one who makes holy and the ones that are made holy are of the same family – by death, he might destroy him holds the power of death that is the devil – and free those who were held in slavery by the fear of death – because he himself suffered when he was tempted he is able to help those who are being tempted

3. fix your thoughts on Jesus the apostle and high priest whom we confess – every house is built by someone, but God is the builder of everything, and we are his house – see to it that none of you has a sinful, unbelieving heart that turns from the living God – encourage each other daily – people died in the desert and were not able to enter because of their unbelief

4. be careful that none of you to be fallen short of it – the message they heard had no value because they did not combine it with faith – the word of God is Living and active – sharper than any double-edged sword it cuts to dividing soul and spirit … it judges thoughts and attitudes of the heart – we have a high priest that was tempted in every way just as we and yet did not sin –

5. Jesus learned obedience from what he suffered, and once made perfect, he became the source of eternal salvation – we have much to say, but it is hard to explain because you are slow to learn – by this time, you ought to be teachers you need someone to teach you – you need milk not solid food – solid food is for the mature who by constant use have trained themselves to distinguish good from evil

6. <u>let us leave the elementary teachings about Christ not laying the foundation again of repentance, faith in God, instruction about baptism, laying on of hands, resurrection, and eternal judgment</u> – **IT IS IMPOSSIBLE TO BRING BACK THOSE WHO FALL AWAY - TO REPENTANCE BECAUSE TO THEIR LOSS**

THEY ARE CRUCIFYING THE SON OF GOD ALL OVER AGAIN AND SUBJECTING HIM TO PUBLIC DISGRACE – God is not unjust – he will remember your work and love for people – do not become lazy imitate those who through faith and patience inherit what was promised – it is impossible for god to lie – he has become a high priest in the order of Melchizedek

7. Melchizedek remains a priest forever – **HOW GREAT HE WAS EVEN ABRAHAM GAVE HIM A TENTH OF THE PLUNDER** – <u>the lesser person is blest by the greater</u> – **WHEN MELCHIZEDEK AND ABRAHAM MEET LEVI WAS STILL IN THE BODY OF HIS ANCESTOR** – why was there a need for another priest to come not in the order of Aaron – **THERE IS A CHANGE IN PRIESTHOOD THERE IS A CHANGE IN LAW** – the lord descended from Judah, and in regard to that tribe Moses said nothing about priests – one who has become a priest not on the basis of regulation but on the basis of the power of an indestructible life – the law made nothing perfect – because Jesus lives forever he has a permanent priesthood – those who come to God he lives to intercede for them – unlike the other high priest he does not need to offer sacrifices day after day first for himself – he sacrificed for their sins once and for all –

8. he does have a high priest and serves in the true tabernacle set up by the Lord – They serve at a sanctuary that is a copy and shadow of what is in heaven – If there was nothing wrong with the first covenant, then no place would have been sought for another – "new" covenant – they will know me –

9. the ark contained manna, Aaron's staff, stone tablets – one high priest entered the inner room and only once a year – the gifts and sacrifices were not able to clear the conscience of the worshipper – external regulations applied until the time of the new order – the blood of Christ – how much more then will the blood of Christ who through the eternal Spirit offered himself unblemished to God cleanse our consciences from acts that lead to death so that we may serve the living God - the law requires that nearly everything be cleansed with blood – without the shedding of blood there is no forgiveness it was necessary for the copies of the heavenly things to be purified – but now he has appeared once for all – man is destined to die once so Christ was sacrificed once he will appear a second time to bring salvation to those who are waiting for him

10. the law is the shadow of the good things that are coming – not the realities themselves – Sacrifices can't make you perfect if they could why were the offered year after year – sacrifices are an annual reminder of sins – we have been made holy through the sacrifice of the body of Christ once and for all – by one sacrifice he has made perfect forever those who are being made holy – sins I will remember no more and where these have been forgiven there is no longer any sacrifice for sin – let us consider how we may spur one another on toward love and good deeds – let us not give up meeting together as some are in the habit of doing – How much severely do think a man deserves to be punished that tramples the Son of God who has treated as unholy the blood of the covenant and who has insulted the spirit – you sympathized with those in prison and joyfully accepted the confiscation of your property because you knew that you yourselves had better and lasting possessions – we are not of those who shrink back and are destroyed but of those who believe and are saved

11. **BY FAITH** Abraham – Faith is being sure of what we hope for… - without faith, it is impossible to please god because anyone that comes to him must believe he exists – people were still living by faith when they died; they had not received what had been promised – God is not ashamed to be called their God – list of how some died sawed in two, stoned, etc., - the world is not worthy of them – these were all commended for their faith, but none received what had been promised

12. **WE ARE SURROUNDED BY A GREAT WALL OF WITNESSES. LET US THROW OFF EVERYTHING THAT HINDERS AND THE SIN THAT SO EASILY ENTANGLES** … the Lord disciplines those he loves – **ENDURE HARDSHIP AS DISCIPLINE** – no discipline seems pleasant at the time, but painful – make every effort to live in peace with all men and be holy without holiness no one will see God see to it that no one misses the grace of the Lord – you have come to mount Zion the heavenly Jerusalem … see to it that you do not refuse him who speaks – <u>let us be thankful and so worship God acceptably with reverence and awe for our God is a consuming fire</u>

13. do not forget to entertain strangers; some have entertained angels – remember those imprisoned – marriage should be honored by all – keep your lives free from the love of money – be content with what you have – remember your leaders… imitate their faith – do not be

carried away by all kinds of strange teachings It is good for our hearts to be strengthened by grace – blood is carried to the holiest place, but bodies burned outside camp same happened to Jesus – let us continually offer to God as a sacrifice of praise the fruit of our lips that confess his name – do not forget to do good and share with others such sacrifices please God – submit to authority Obey them so there work will be a joy and not a burden for what advantage would that be to you – pray for us – live honorably in every way – Jesus will equip you with every good thing for doing his will- may he work in us what is pleasing to him

James

1. **CONSIDER IT PURE JOY WHEN YOU FACE TRIALS – TESTING OF YOUR FAITH BRINGS PERSEVERANCE** - perseverance must finish its work to make you mature – blessed is the man who perseveres under trial – **NO ONE SHOULD SAY GOD IS TEMPTING ME** – each is tempted when by his own evil desire is dragged away and enticed – after desire is conceived it gives birth to sin and sin to death – every good and perfect gift comes from above – he chose to give us birth through the word of truth that we might be a kind of first fruits – everyone should be quick to listen, slow to speak, slow to anger – get rid of all filth and accept the word that has been planted in you which can save you – **DO NOT JUST LISTEN TO THE WORD DO WHAT IT SAYS!!** – look intently into the perfect law which gives freedom – can't be religious and have a loose tongue – **PURE AND FAULTLESS RELIGION IS THIS LOOK AFTER ORPHANS AND WIDOWS AND KEEP ONESELF FROM BEING POLLUTED BY THE WORLD**

2. **DON'T SHOW FAVORITISM – YOU INSULT THE POOR** – the royal law – love your neighbor… - whoever keeps the whole law but stumbles on one point is guilty of the whole law – speak and act as one going to trial – mercy triumphs over judgment – **WHAT GOOD… IF A MAN HAS FAITH WITHOUT DEEDS? - SOMEONE IS STARVING, AND YOU DO NOT HELP – FAITH BY ITSELF IF NOT ACCOMPANIED BY ACTION IS DEAD – I WILL SHOW YOU MY FAITH BY WHAT I DO** – His (Abrahams) faith and his actions were working together, and his faith was made complete by what he did – **A PERSON IS JUSTIFIED BY WHAT HE DOES AND NOT BY FAITH ALONE** – as the body is dead without spirit so is faith without deeds

3. **NOT MANY OF YOUR SHOULD PRESUME TO BE TEACHERS – THOSE WHO TEACH WILL BE JUDGED MORE STRICTLY** – we all stumble in many ways – the tongue is a small part of the body, but it makes great boasts – **A SPARK CAN START A GREAT FIRE – THE TONGUE IS ALSO A FIRE** – no man can tame the tongue – with the tongue we praise God and curse man – can both fresh and saltwater flow from the same stream

145

– WHO IS WISE AND UNDERSTANDING LET HIM SHOW IT BY HIS GOOD LIFE AND DEEDS DONE IN HUMILITY – wisdom is pure, peace-loving, considerate, submissive, full of mercy and good fruit, impartial and sincere –

4. fights and quarrels come from your desires that battle within you – **YOU DO NOT HAVE BECAUSE YOU DO NOT ASK WHEN YOU ASK YOU DO NOT HAVE** – friendship with the world is hatred toward God – God gives grace to the humble – Submit to God resist the devil - Come near to god, and he will come near to you – do not slander one another – **YOU OUGHT TO SAY "IF IT IS THE LORD'S WILL I WILL…." ANYONE THE WHO KNOWS THE GOOD HE OUGHT TO DO AND DOESN'T DO IT SINS**

5. you rich people weep and will – Don't grumble against each other – as an example of suffering look to the prophets – Job's perseverance – **LET YOUR YES BE YES, AND YOUR NO BE NO** – is anyone in trouble he should pray – happy pray – sick call the elders – he will be made well and his sins forgiven – **CONFESS YOUR SINS TO ONE ANOTHER AND PRAY FOR EACH OTHER SO THAT YOU MAY BE HEALED** – the prayer of a righteous man is powerful and effective – whoever turns a sinner from the error of his ways will save him from death

I Peter

1. To God's elect <u>strangers in the world</u> – who have been chosen according to the foreknowledge of God for obedience – **YOU HAVE SUFFERED IN ALL KINDS OF TRIALS. THESE HAVE COME SO YOUR FAITH MAY BE PROVED GENUINE AND RESULT IN PRAISE, GLORY, AND HONOR** – <u>you have not seen him, you love him – you believe him – and are filled with an inexpressible and glorious joy –</u> the goal of faith is salvation – **THE PROPHETS SPOKE OF THE GRACE THAT WAS TO COME TO YOU** – they were not serving themselves but you – prepare you minds for action be self-controlled set your hope on the grace to be given to you – be holy in all you do – <u>live as strangers here –</u> **YOU HAVE PURIFIED YOURSELVES BY OBEYING THE TRUTH SO THAT YOU HAVE SINCERE LOVE FOR YOUR BROTHER LOVE ONE ANOTHER DEEPLY FROM THE HEART YOU HAVE BEEN BORN AGAIN NOT OF PERISHABLE SEED** – the word of the lord stands forever

2. crave spiritual milk – like living stones are being built into a spiritual house – **OFFER SPIRITUAL SACRIFICES ACCEPTABLE TO GOD** – they stumble because that is what they are destined for – you are a chosen people belonging to God – <u>I urge you to be as aliens and strangers of this world</u> – live such good lives among the pagans … - Submit to authorities – <u>live as free men but do not use your freedom as a cover-up for evil-</u> show proper respect for everyone – love the brotherhood of believers – slaves submit to your masters – when they hurled their insults at him he did not retaliate when he suffered he made no threats –

3. wives submit to husbands – so they are won over without words but actions – **YOUR BEAUTY SHOULD BE THAT OF THE INNER SELF, THE UNFADING BEAUTY OF A GENTLE AND QUIT SPIRIT** – <u>husbands be considerate of your wife- weaker partner – so nothing will hinder your prayers</u> – **LIVE IN HARMONY, BE SYMPATHETIC, LOVE AS BROTHERS, BE COMPASSIONATE AND HUMBLE** - repay insult and evil with blessing – <u>the eyes of the Lord are on the righteous and his prayers are attentive to their prayer</u> – who is going to harm you if you are

doing good? – **ALWAYS BE PREPARED TO GIVE AN ANSWER TO THE REASON YOU HAVE HOPE BUT DO SO WITH GENTLENESS AND RESPECT** – Christ also went and preached to the spirits in prison – Noah's boat now **SYMBOLIZES BAPTISM THAT NOW SAVES YOU** – It saves you by the resurrection of Jesus Christ

4. he who has suffered in the body is done with sin; as a result, he does not live the rest of his earthly life for evil human desires but the will of God – the gospel was preached even to those who are now dead – **BE CLEAR MINDED AND SELF-CONTROLLED SO THAT YOU CAN PRAY** – love covers a multitude of sins – **IF ANYONE SPEAKS HE SHOULD DO SO AS ONE SPEAKING THE VERY WORDS OF GOD – SERVE WITH THE STRENGTH OF GOD IF YOU SUFFER AS A CHRISTIAN DO NOT BE ASHAMED** – it is hard for the righteous to be saved what will become of the ungodly and the sinner – commit to the faithful Creator and continue to do good –

5. to the elders, be shepherds of the flock – do so not because you must but because you are willing – young men, be submissive – humble yourself – **CAST YOUR ANXIETY ON HIM BECAUSE HE CARES FOR YOU** – be self-controlled and alert the devil prowls around like a lion looking for someone to devour

II Peter

1. **MAKE EVERY EFFORT TO ADD TO YOUR FAITH GOODNESS, GOODNESS KNOWLEDGE...SELF-CONTROL...PERSEVERANCE...GODLINESS...KINDNESS ...LOVE** – if any does not have them, he is nearsighted and blind and has forgotten that he has been cleansed from his past sins – **FOR IF YOU DO ALL OF THESE THINGS, YOU WILL NEVER FAIL –**

2. <u>there were false prophets among the people just as there will be false teachers among you</u> – in their greed, they will exploit you – <u>God did not spare angels when they sinned; he did not spare the ancient world</u> – <u>Lot</u> was tormented day after day in Sodom by the lawless deeds he saw and heard – bold and arrogant these men are not afraid to slander celestial things – even angel (stronger and more powerful) don't slander in front of the Lord – they blaspheme in matters they don't understand – **THEIR IDEA OF PLEASURE IS TO CAROUSE IN BROAD DAYLIGHT – WITH EYES FULL OF ADULTERY THEY NEVER STOP SINNING THEY SEDUCE THE UNSTABLE** – experts in greed have left the straightway and wandered off to follow Balaam – by appealing to the lustful desires of sinful human nature they entice people who are just escaping - **THEY PROMISE FREEDOM WHILE THEY THEMSELVES ARE SLAVES OF DEPRAVITY FOR A MAN IS SLAVE TO WHATEVER HAS MASTERED HIM** – it would be better if they had never obeyed the gospel

3. in the last days will be scoffers saying where is this 'coming' – with the Lord, a day is like a thousand years and a thousand years like a day – **HE IS PATIENT WITH YOU NOT WANTING ANY TO PERISH** – the day of the Lord will come like a thief – make every effort to be blameless – **THE LORD'S PATIENCE MEANS SALVATION** – Paul wrote some things that are hard to understand and many people distort – be on your guard

I John

1. we have seen and touched Jesus – the life appeared, we have seen it and testified to it, and we proclaim to you eternal life – God is light in him; there is no darkness – if we claim fellowship with him but walk in darkness we lie and do not live by the truth – but if we walk in the light we have fellowship – if we claim to be without sin we deceive ourselves – **IF WE CONFESS OUR SINS HE IS FAITHFUL AND JUST AND WILL FORGIVE US AND PURIFY US** – if we claim to be without sin we make him out to be a liar – and his word has no place in us

2. if anybody does sin, we have one who speaks to the Father in our defense – he is the atoning sacrifice for our sins – **THE MAN WHO SAYS, I KNOW HIM BUT DOES NOT DO WHAT HE COMMANDS, IS A LIAR, AND THE TRUTH IS NOT IN HIM** – if anybody obeys the word God's love is made complete in him this is how we know we are in him live and walk as Christ – anyone who claims to be in the light but hates his brother is still in the darkness – **THE WORD OF GOD LIVES IN YOU** – Do not love the world or anything in it – **CRAVINGS OF THE SINFUL MAN, LUST OF HIS EYES, BOASTING OF WHAT HE HAS OR DOES COMES NOT FROM THE FATHER, BUT FROM THE WORLD** – many antichrists have come – no lie comes from the truth – antichrist man who denies the Father and the son – his anointing teaches you about all things

3. **HOW GREAT IS GOD'S LOVE THAT WE ARE EVEN CALLED CHILDREN OF GOD** – what we will become has not yet been made known – sin is lawlessness – no one who lives in him continues to sin – he who does what is right is righteous – just as he is righteous – he who keeps on sinning is of the devil – the reason the son of man appeared was to destroy the devil's work – **BECAUSE GOD'S SEED REMAINS IN HIM HE CANNOT KEEP ON SINNING** – this is the message you heard from the begin we should love one another – do not be surprised if the world hates you – **ANYONE WHO DOES NOT LOVE REMAINS IN DEATH** – this is how we know what love is Christ lay his life down for us we should do the same – **IF ANY ONE HAS MATERIAL THINGS AND SEES A BROTHER IN NEED BUT HAS NO PITY ON**

HIM HOW CAN THE LOVE OF GOD BE IN HIM – LET US NOT LOVE WITH WORDS BUT WITH ACTIONS AND TRUTH – if our hearts do not condemn us we have confidence before God and receive anything we ask – this is his command to believe in his Son Jesus and to love one another as he commanded us – **THOSE WHO OBEY LIVE IN HIM AND HE IN THEM** – we know it by the spirit he gave us

4. **EVERY SPIRIT THAT ACKNOWLEDGES THAT JESUS CHRIST HAS COME IN THE FLESH IS FROM GOD** – from the world and speak from the viewpoint of the world and the world listens to them – we are from God and whoever knows God listens to us – **GOD IS LOVE** – everyone that has been born of God and knows God knows love comes from God – he sent his one and only son into the world that we might live since God loved us we ought to love others – **IF ANYONE ACKNOWLEDGES THAT JESUS IS THE SON OF GOD, GOD LIVES IN HIM AND HE IN GOD-** if we love one another his love is made complete in us – **WE KNOW AND RELY ON THE LOVE GOD HAS FOR US** – whoever lives in love lives in God – **THERE IS NO FEAR IN LOVE – WE HAVE CONFIDENCE ON THE DAY OF JUDGMENT BECAUSE OF LOVE -** we love because he first loved us – "I love god" but hates his brother is a liar –

5. this is how we know we are children of God; by loving God and carrying out his commands – love of God = Obeying his commands – who overcomes the world only he who believes that Jesus is the son of God – this is the one who came by Blood and water – he did not come by water only but by blood – these three testify the spirit the blood and water – God has given us eternal life, and this life is in the son – he who has the son has life – I write these things to those who believe so that you may know that you have eternal life- if we ask anything he will give us – if anyone sees a brother do a sin that does not lead to death he should pray for him – there is sin that does not lead to death – we know that anyone in God does not sin – know – the world is under the control of the evil one – know – the son of God has come and has given us understanding so that we may know him who is true

2 John

To the Chosen lady and her children – and this is love that we walk in obedience to his commands – if anyone comes and does not bring this teaching, do not take him into the house or welcome him

3 John

To my friend Gaius – I wrote to the church, but Diotrephes who loves to be first will have nothing to do with us – do not imitate what is evil but what is good

Jude

Brother of James – mercy, peace, and love be yours in abundance – godless men change the grace of god into a license for immorality and deny Jesus Christ, our only Sovereign and Lord – these dreamers pollute their own bodies reject authority and slander celestial beings – they are blemishes at your love feasts – **THEY ARE GRUMBLERS AND FAULT FINDERS FOLLOWING THEIR OWN EVIL DESIRES, THEY BOAST ABOUT THEMSELVES** and flatter others for their own advantage – they follow mere natural instincts and do not have the spirit – build yourselves up in your most holy faith and pray in the Holy Spirit – keep yourselves in God's love as you wait – be merciful to those who doubt snatch others from the fire and save them – to others show mercy mixed with fear – hating even the clothing stained by sin – to him who is able to keep you from falling and to present you before his glorious presence without fault and great joy

Revelation

1. Made known by sending his angel to his servant John – To him who loves us and has freed us from our sins by his blood and has made us to be a kingdom and priests to serve his God and Father – On the lord's day – I am the living one I was dead and behold I am alive forever and ever! And I hold the keys of death and Hades – Seven stars are angels of the seven churches

2. **CHURCH IN EPHESUS** – Remember the height from which you have fallen! Repent! – **CHURCH IN SMYRNA** – I know your afflictions and poverty, yet you are rich – they slander you who say they are Jews and are not but are a synagogue of Satan – **CHURCH IN PERGAMUM** - Repent – To him who overcomes I will give some hidden manna – I will also give a white stone with a new name on it – **CHURCH IN THYATIRA** – you are doing more than you did at first nevertheless you tolerate that woman Jezebel – Hold on what you have until I come

3. **CHURCH IN SARDIS** – you have a reputation for being alive, but you are dead – your deeds are not complete in the sight of God – you have a few that have not soiled their clothes – **CHURCH IN PHILADELPHIA** – you have kept my word and not denied my name – **CHURCH IN LAODICEA – YOU ARE NEITHER HOT NOR COLD SO I WILL SPIT YOU OUT OF MY MOUTH** – you acquired wealth and say I do not need a thing – you do not realize that you are wretched pitiful, blind, and naked – those whom I rebuke and discipline I Love

4. The throne of heaven – same creatures as in Daniel

5. The Scroll and the Lamb – you are worthy of taking the scroll and of opening its seals because with your blood you purchased men for God…

6. The seven seals opened – saints told to wait to be avenged until the rest that was to be killed had been as they were

7. 144,000 sealed – a great multitude that no one could count … they were wearing white robes

8. the seventh seal opens the seven trumpets

9. Many were killed – the number of the mounted troops was 200,000,000. I heard their number **"THE REST OF MANKIND THAT WERE NOT KILLED BY THESE PLAGUES STILL DID NOT REPENT... THEY DID NOT STOP WORSHIPPING DEMONS... NOR DID THEY REPENT OF THEIR MURDERS, MAGIC ARTS, THEIR SEXUAL IMMORALITY, OR THEIR THEFTS."**

10. angel and the scroll

11. the two witnesses – the seventh trumpet

12. woman and the dragon – the great dragon was hurled down – that ancient serpent called the devil or Satan who leads the whole world astray and his angels with him – the dragon made war against the rest of her offspring, those who obey God's commandments and hold to the testimony of Jesus

13. beast of the sea – beast out of the earth

14. the lamb and the 144,000; these are those who did not defile themselves with women, for they kept themselves pure – They follow the lamb wherever he goes – they were purchased from among men and offered as first fruits to God and the Lamb. No lie was found in their mouths; they were blameless – 3 angels -blessed are the dead who die in the Lord from now on – they will rest from their labor, for their deeds will follow them.

15. 7 angels 7 plagues

16. Seven Bowls of God's wrath – Behold, I come like a thief!

17. Woman on the beast – that woman was drunk with the blood of the saints – and with him will be his called, chosen, and faithful followers

18. **FALL OF BABYLON – MERCHANTS WERE SAD BECAUSE NO ONE BUYS THEIR CARGOES ANYMORE – NO MORE TRADE, INCLUDING "BODIES AND SOULS OF MEN"**

19. Hallelujah! – I fell to worship the angel, and he said don't do it! – Worship God – his name is the word of God

20. for thousand years – I saw thrones on which were seated those who were given authority, and I saw the souls of those who had been beheaded because of the testimony for Jesus – they came to life and reigned with Jesus for a thousand years the rest of the dead did not

come to life until after the thousand years – the sea, death, and Hades gave up the dead then death and Hades were thrown into the lake of fire

21. New Jerusalem – now the dwelling of God is with men, and he will live with them – **I DID NOT SEE A TEMPLE IN THE CITY BECAUSE THE LORD AND THE LAMB ARE ITS TEMPLE**

22. the river of life – there will be no more night for the Lord God will give them light – Jesus is coming – I am coming soon – I fell at the feet of the angel – do not do it – worship God – the spirit and the bride say come and let him who hears say come

Made in United States
North Haven, CT
01 August 2024

55642150R00089